EDUCATION AND GLOBALISATION

By
Dr. M. Lakshmi Narasaiah
M.A., Ph.D.
Professor of Economics
Co-ordinator, Dept. of M.B.A. and Commerce
Special Officer
Sri Krishnadevaraya University Post-graduate Centre
Kurnool–518 002
Andhra Pradesh
(India)

D P H

DISCOVERY PUBLISHING HOUSE PVT. LTD.
NEW DELHI-110 002

Published by:
Namit Wasan

DISCOVERY PUBLISHING HOUSE PVT. LTD.
4383/4B, Ansari Road, Darya Ganj
New Delhi-110 002 (India)
Phone : +91-11-23279245; 23253475; 43596065
E-mail : discoverybooksindia@gmail.com
discoverypublishinghouse@gmail.com
namitwasan9@gmail.com
web : www.discoverypublishinggroup.com

***Edition:* 2020**

ISBN: 978-81-8356-311-6

Education and Globalisation

Printed at:
Infinity Imaging Systems
Delhi

Preface

Globalisation has become today's buzzword. It has also become a battle ground for two radically opposed groups. There are the anti-globalists, who fear globalisation and stress only its downside, seeking therefore powerful interventions aimed at taming, if not (unwittingly) crippling it. Then there are the "globalist" (a class to which I belong) who celebrate globalisation instead, emphasize its upside, while seeking only to ensure that its few rough edges be handled through appropriate policies that serve to make globalisation yet more attractive.

Many anti-globalists consider the central problem of globalisation to be its amorality, or even its immorality. But these critics have too blanket an approach to globalisation. The word covers a variety of phenomena that characterize an integrating world economy: trade, short-term capital flows, direct foreign investment, immigration, cultural convergence *et al.* The sins of one of the above cannot be visited upon the virtues of another. Some are benign even when largely unregulated whereas others can be fatal if left wholly to the marketplace.

In particular, the freeing of trade is largely benign: if I exchange some of my toothpaste for some of your toothbrushes, we will both be better off than if we did not trade at all. It would require a wild imagination, and a deranged mind, to think that such freeing of trade leads to debilitating economic crises. Equally, it is illogical to believe, as non-economists who fear globalisation do, that freeing of trade is bad because the freeing of short-term capital flows led to a debilitating financial and economic crises and could do so again. In fact, while there are some obvious simulates between free trade and free capital flows, e.g. that segmentation of markets creates efficiency losses—the economic and political dissimilarities are even more compelling and policy-makers cannot ignore them.

Dr. M. Lakshmi Narasaiah

Contents

Chapter 1

The Nation-State and Globalisation

The world has changed dramatically. Some of the changes are as yet only dimly understood. We are all going to be confronted with many challenges to the whole concept of government and to the role of the nation-state as we move into the next century.

There are two principal aspects to these changes. Globalisation of the world economies is sharply limiting the independence of action of the nation-state. In addition, we are only just beginning to understand what the existence of one superpower, supreme militarily, financially, means to the evolution of world diplomacy and world politics.

These remarks are directed to the first aspect. Governments are now losing influence. Private enterprise, capitalism, summarised as 'the market', is gaining power. Privatisation is a keyword. Across the political spectrum, liberal conservative and formerly socialist parties have all accepted the downsizing of government, the privatisation of many activities and the reduction of government debt. Governments in crisis in the developed or in the developing world have been left in no doubt about what they should do.

The International Monetary Fund and the World Bank have made it clear that assistance would not be available to countries in distress unless appropriate policies were put in place, and IMF prescriptions often involve substantial and detailed micro-economic reform within a country with considerable hardship for its people.

Meanwhile, competition for international capital has become much more severe. In the early independence years, Commonwealth countries believed they could write their own internal rules about the performance and behaviour of capital. Now those rules have to be rewritten to maximize international attraction. The relationship has to be competitive; the rules have to be friendly to capital. This is a totally different environment from the one in which most Commonwealth countries gained their independence in the immediate post-war years.

The new global organisation of industry has significant consequences for social policy. Many governments would have conducted policies designed to see that workers gained a fair share of the returns of an enterprise. With the globalisation of industry, such policies are no longer possible. Governments now tend to argue for lower wages, for smaller workforces, to maximize the competitiveness of their particular country as a home for global corporations. This has consequences of enhancing the profit share as opposed to the wage share of a particular enterprise.

One direct consequence of these changes is a significantly growing disparity in wealth between rich and poor in all countries worldwide. This may not matter so much if the poor were also becoming better off compared to their own earlier standards but in many cases this is not so. The idea of a living wage is no longer relevant. Workers in some countries are often paid a wage which could not support even the smallest of families. In this day, if that is what the market determines, then that is what must happen.

In today's world, governments must fashion their policies to meet the wishes of the international marketplace.

There are fundamental differences from earlier times. The global organisation of industry in which national boundaries become irrelevant is certainly new. Some aspects of information technology can operate much faster and with more devastating effect than the old cable system of the last hundred years. This has led to an explosive growth in financial markets. The volume of money traded each day is huge (and) through modern communications, this finance has great mobility.

We all know enough of markets to know that they favour the powerful, the united and the strong and that markets can overwhelm and destroy smaller players. Sometimes smaller players are entire nations.

Those who suggest that the markets alone must be allowed to determine economic outcomes favour a world in which the large will do much better than the small. So far as countries are concerned, most Commonwealth countries are in the smaller category in a world in which large financial institutions and manufacturing corporations operating globally will dominate trade and commerce.

For most countries, banks and financial institutions, which are part of the culture of that country, will become a matter of the past. Banking services will be American, European, Japanese or perhaps Chinese. The consequences of this market dominance are clear. Corporations need a global spread and many national rules for the good order and conduct of business and commerce will no longer be relevant.

For the world as a whole, the most serious problem is volatility, possibly leading to systematic breakdown. Since the Asian economic problems of 1997, there has been a great deal of discussion about the present system and about changes that need to be made.

For a while it appeared that the United States really was going to move the reform process forward but now the tendency seem to be 'it's all right, we have escaped, leave well enough alone' ...There is a need to reform the system, to establish much tougher international rules for prudential supervision and control. The IMF has demonstrated time and time again that it is not interested in avoiding crises, it is only interested in picking up the pieces after they have occurred. If this is its charter, it certainly needs reviewing. The IMF's present operations are inadequate.

Since governments have seemingly lost significant power to corporations and to financial markets and since they do operate within an increasingly globalised framework, individual governments are not capable of undertaking this task. The task is international and global. Whether it is a reformed IMF or a new institution is a matter for debate.

At their last meeting the Commonwealth Finance Ministers pointed to a number of changes, most of which are desirable, but there was no sense of great urgency, no sense of dynamism. They spoke of a need for new financial market architecture but nobody has tried to spell out what that means.

There are two specific tasks: how to preserve some form of equity and reasonable competition in a globalised market-place and how to establish stability within the financial markets themselves.

The IMF's financial resources should be strengthened as a means of averting crises through the provision of contingency funds. Immediate access to adequate funding can be essential for this purpose if crises are to be avoided. Finding a way to encourage the IMF to help avert crises instead of just reacting to crises after they have occurred is a most important requirement.

In any liquidity arrangement, assisting a country is distress, the IMF should take care not to absolve lenders of their responsibility. In some cases IMF should take care not to absolve lenders of their responsibility. In some cases IMF bailouts have done more to help the lenders than the countries themselves. The lenders need to carry their own risk.

For poor countries, how to protect themselves and advance the welfare of their own people in an unpredictable world is a major challenge and very often a major problem. Apart from moves to establish greater stability designed to avoid systematic breakdown within the world's financial system, there also need to be urgent moves to establish an international body to establish rules for fair trading in a globalised environment. Middle ranking and small countries would have most to gain from such an innovation.

Chapter 2

The Truth About Global Competition
The Economic Myths Behind Globalisation

Local communities everywhere are on the frontlines of what might well be characterised as World War III. It is not the nuclear confrontation between East and West—between the Soviet Union and the United States—that we once feared. It is a very different kind of conflict. There is no clash of competing military forces and the struggle is not defined by national borders. But it does involve an often violent struggle for control of physical resources and territory that is destroying lives and communities at every hand. It is a struggle between the forces and institutions of economic globalisation and the communities that are trying to reclaim control of their economic lives. It is a conflict between competing goals—economic growth to maximize profits for absentee owners versus creating healthy communities that are good places for people to live. It is a competition for the control of markets and resources between global corporations and financial markets on the one hand and locally owned businesses serving local markets on the other.

Two things of fundamental importance to each and everyone of us are now very much at stake.

- Will people and communities control their local resources and economies and be able to set their own goals and priorities based on their own values and aspiration? Or will these decisions be left to global financial markets and corporations that are blind to all values save one—instant financial returns?

- Will the life sustaining resources produced by the regenerative capacities of our planet's eco-systems be equitably shared to provide for the material needs of all of us who inhabit this bountiful planet, as well as for our children and their children unto the seventh generation and beyond? Or will we allow a global economic system that is now functioning on auto-pilot beyond conscious human control to consume and destroy the eco-system and our social fabric in its insatiable quest for money?

Economists, politicians, corporate spokespersons and the media have for years been touting the benefits of the global economy. They have called on us to support trade agreements such as the North American Free Trade Agreement (NAFTA) and the World Trade Organisation (WTO) to remove the constraints of economic borders and open to everyone the opportunities of growth and prosperity in the global economy. They have promised rich rewards for those workers and communities that become successful global competitors.

Many of the most ardent boosters of economic globalisation met earlier in the year at the annual meeting of the World Economic Forum. This Forum has for years brought together top industrialists and political figures from around the world to advance the proposition that removing tariffs and other restrictions on the free international flow of trade and money is a key to creating new economic opportunity and prosperity. It thus caused quite a stir when the Forum publicly announced that economic globalisation is producing disastrous consequences that threaten the political stability of the Western democracies. Their warning bears close examination for being one of the most honest and accurate assessments of the consequences of economic globalisation yet produced by leading advocates of that process. The observation is that:

- Economic globalisation is causing severe economic dislocation and social instability.
- The technological changes of the past few years have eliminated more jobs than they have created.
- The global competition "that is part and parcel of globalisation leads to winner-take-all situations; those who come out on top win big, and the losers lose even bigger."
- Higher profits no longer mean more job security and better wages. "Globalisation tends to delink the fate of the corporation from the fate of its employees."
- Unless serious corrective action is taken soon, the backlash could destabilize the Western democracies.

We don't have to go far to find examples of what they are talking about and why people are getting a bit upset as they wake up to the realities of who is winning in the ruthless competition of the global economy. The disparities between the winners and losers in the global competition are becoming more obscene with each passing day.

We are coming to realize that the extravagant promises of the advocates of the global economy are based on a number of myths that have become so deeply embedded in Western industrial culture that we have grown to accept them without examination.

- The myth that growth in GNP is a valid measure of human well-being and progress.
- The myth that free unregulated markets efficiently allocate a society's resources.
- The myth that growth in trade benefits ordinary people.
- The myth that global corporations are benevolent institutions that if freed from governmental interference will provide a clean environment for all and good jobs for the poor.
- The myth that absentee investors create local prosperity.

The Growth Myth

Our measures of growth are deeply flawed in that they are purely measures of activity in the monetised economy. Expanded use of cigarettes and alcohol increases economic output both as a direct consequence of their consumption and because of the related increase in health care needs. The need to clean up oil spills generates economic activity. Gun sales to minors generate economic activity. A divorce generates both lawyers fees and the need to buy or rent and outfit a new home increasing real estate brokerage fees and retail sales. It is now well documented that in number of other countries the quality of living of ordinary people has been declining as aggregate economic output increases.

The growth myth has another serious flaw. Since 1950, the world's economic output has increased 5 to 7 times. That growth has already increased the human burden on the planet's regenerative systems—its soils, air, water, fisheries, and forestry systems—beyond what the planet can sustain. Continuing to press for economic growth beyond the planet's sustainable limits does two things. It accelerates the rate of breakdown of the earth's regenerative systems—as we see so dramatically demonstrated in the case of many ocean fisheries, and it intensifies the competition between rich and poor for the resource base that remains.

This is vividly illustrated by many of the development projects in India many funded with loans from the World Bank and other multilateral development banks—that displace the poor so that the lands and waters on which they depend for their livelihood can be converted to uses that generate higher economic returns—meaning converted to use by people who can pay more than those who are displaced.

The Myth of Free Unregulated Markets

It is almost inherent in the nature of markets that their efficient function depends on the presence of a strong government to set a framework of rules for their operation. We know that free markets create monopolies, which government must break up to maintain the conditions of competition on which market function depends.

We also know that markets only allocate efficiently when prices reflect the full and true costs of production. Yet in the absence of governmental regulation, market incentives persistently push firms to cut corners on safety, pay workers less than a living wages, and dump untreated toxic discharges into a convenient river. In our present competitive context if management does not take such measures, they are likely to be replaced by the owners or bought out by someone with less scruples who will.

The Myth of Free Trade

Many so-called trade agreements, such as the North American Free Trade Agreement (NAFTA) and the World Trade Organisation (WTO) are not really trade agreements at all. They are economic integration agreements intended to guarantee the rights of global corporations to move both goods and investments wherever they wish—free from public interference and accountability. WTO is best described as a bill of rights for global corporations.

The Myth that Economic Globalisation is Inevitable

Many of the people who claim globalisation is a consequence of inevitable historical forces are paid to promote that message by the same global corporations that have invested millions of dollars in advancing the globalisation policy agenda.

The Myth that Corporations are Benevolent Institutions

The corporation is an institutional invention specifically and internationally created to concentrate control over economic resources while shielding those who hold the resulting power from liability for the consequences of its use. The more national economies become integrated into a seamless global economy, the further corporate power extends beyond the reach of any state and the less accountable it becomes to any human interest or institution other than a global financial system that is now best described as a gigantic legal gambling casino.

All over the world people are indeed waking up to the truth about economic globalisation and are taking steps to reclaim and rebuild their local economies. Such communities face basic choices as to how they will divide their efforts between competing for a share of the declining pool of good jobs that global corporations offer and working to create locally owned enterprises that sustainably harvest and process local resources to produce the jobs and the goods and services that local people need to live healthy, happy, and fulfilling lives in balance with the environment.

Our experience with the real consequences of economic globalisation is pointing to many important lessons. One such lesson is that economies should be local, rooting power in the people and communities who realize their well-being depends on the health and vitality of their local ecosystem. If it is protectionist to favour local firms and workers who pay local taxes, live by local rules, respect and nurture the local ecosystems, compete fairly in local markets, and contribute to community life—then let us all proudly proclaim ourselves to be protectionist.

Such choices are not isolationist. To the contrary, they create a foundation for creative cooperation with our neighbours—whether they be in the United States or in other countries—to share experience, ideas and technology—and to join in international solidarity in rewriting the rules of the global economy to favour local over global businesses, and to encourage cooperative relations among people and communities. It is our consciousness—our ways of thinking and our sense of membership in a larger community—not our economies—that should be global.

Millions of people are also making an important discovery—that life is about living—not consuming. A life of material sufficiency can be filled with social, cultural, intellectual, and spiritual abundance that place no burden on the planet.

It is time to assume responsibility for creating a new human future of just and sustainable communities freed from the myth that greed, competition, and mindless consumption are paths to individual and collective fulfillment. It will take millions of people around the world—linked together into a powerful political coalition aimed at radical, political and economic—reform to win the war that global capital is waging against us.

Chapter 3

Globalisation

A Moral Imperative

Globalisation has become today's buzzword. It has also become a battle ground for two radically opposed groups. There are the anti-globalists, who fear globalisation and stress only its downside, seeking therefore powerful interventions aimed at taming, if not (unwittingly) crippling it. Then there are the "globalist" (a class to which I belong) who celebrate globalisation instead, emphasize its upside, while seeking only to ensure that its few rough edges be handled through appropriate policies that serve to make globalisation yet more attractive.

Many anti-globalists consider the central problem of globalisation to be its amorality, or even its immorality. But these critics have too blanket an approach to globalisation. The word covers a variety of phenomena that characterize an integrating world economy: trade, short-term capital flows, direct foreign investment, immigration, cultural convergence et al. The sins of one of the above cannot be visited upon the virtues of another. Some are benign even when largely unregulated whereas others can be fatal if left wholly to the marketplace.

In particular, the freeing of trade is largely benign: if I exchange some of my toothpaste for some of your toothbrushes, we will both be better off than if we did not trade at all. It would require a wild imagination, and a deranged mind, to think that such freeing of trade leads to debilitating economic crises. Equally, it is illogical to believe, as non-economists who fear globalisation do, that freeing of trade is bad because the freeing of short-term capital flows led to a debilitating financial and economic crises and could do so again. In fact, while there are some obvious simulates between free trade and free capital flows, e.g. that segmentation of markets creates efficiency losses—the economic and political dissimilarities are even more compelling and policy-makers cannot ignore them.

Anti-globalist critics are in fact often reacting viscerally to a much larger issue: the victory of capitalism over its arch rival, communism. For campus idealists who have always looked for alternatives to what they conventionally consider to be the greed and lack of social conscience that characterize capitalism, the situation is psychologically intolerable. Some have turned to street theatre, nihilism and the anti-intellectualism that has been manifest in the last few years. The more sophisticated have succumbed to a stereotypical representation of corporation as the evil forces of capitalism that have captured the state, democratic institutions, and even international bodies such as the World Trade Organisation.

What these critics often forget is that certain economic freedoms are basic to prosperity and social well-being under any conditions, and are thus of the highest moral value. Property rights and markets, for instance, provide incentives to produce and allocate resources efficiently, and can in turn strengthen democracy by allowing a means of sustenance outside pervasive government structures. The quality and breadth of democracy can then be enlarged as excluded groups, such as women and the poor, are pulled into literacy, gainful employment and better health through higher public spending or the spread of economic incentives.

Critics nevertheless go on to maintain that the global spread of free markets and free trade is responsible for continuing poverty in poor countries, and for alleged growth in inequality between and within countries. Labour unions in the rich countries also fear that trade in cheap labour-using goods from poor countries.

But I do not think these concerns are well-founded. In India which has almost a quarter of the world's poor, there is good evidence that autarchic and anti-market policies produced abysmally low growth rates at 3.5 per cent annually over a quarter of a century, with a correspondingly negligible impact on poverty has declined. Higher growth rates in turn depend on several factors; but openness to trade and direct investment and a skilful use of markets are definitely and important contributory factor.

As for inequality among nations, it is precisely those countries that embraced integration into the world economy, i.e. the Far Eastern Four and then the ASEAN countries, which raced ahead with dramatic growth rates whereas several countries of Africa, Latin America and Asia that looked inwards failed to deliver growth and also made little dent on poverty.

The evidence on trade and investment impoverishing our workers is also flawed. My own research suggests that the downward pressure on workers' wages due to technical change has been dampened, not magnified, by trade with the poor countries. Research also shows that big corporations use abroad technologies similar to those at home, instead of exploiting lower standards or forcing them yet lower through their financial clout.

One result of these mistaken arguments against globalisation has been an insistent clamour for certain environmental and labour standard to be linked to rules on international trade. But by seeking to create new obstacles to free trade, you undermine the freeing of trade, while mixing up trade with a moral agenda undermines that very moral agenda. It gives other countries the definite impression that you are using ethical rhetoric to mask protectionist self-interest.

The notion that global free trade and investment are responsible for poverty, inequality, lowering of standards and harming social progress is little short of astonishing. Yet national politicians and international bureaucrats give it who think that going along is way of getting along. In denying the virtues of globalisation, they actually harm the very causes they profess to embrace.

Chapter 4

Globalisation and Knowledge Divide

Globalisation looks very different when it is seen, not from the capitals of the West, but from the cities and villages of the South, where most of humanity lives. Four examples taken from India, illustrate how the paradoxical forces shaping globalisation look when seen from the other side.

Five school children died in a remote village in India after drinking water and powdered milk mixed in a vat that had contained a powerful insecticide. Nobody could read the label of the vat and the children were poisoned. The insecticide in question has been banned in practically every industrialised nation; its sale continues only in places like my country.

Secondly, an important annual event recently took place in North India. Potato growers gather there to exchange the best seeds they have produced in the last year. It is an act of pride for communities to share with others seeds that will help improve the production of potatoes. A transnational corporation attended the festival and are now working to patent the genes of these traditional foodstuffs in order to sell them as profit.

India's macro-economic indicators are excellent. In the offices of investment bankers, you will be told that India is a great investment opportunity. The situation is not so rosy, however. Thirty per cent of the population have been living below the poverty line for the last so many years. Ten per cent of the population are living below the critical poverty line: their income is insufficient to pay for even minimal nourishment. So much of the workforce is unemployed or under employed.

A distinguished North American political scientist, Dr. Benjamin Barber, recently pointed out that in the United States democracy had degenerated into bringing one group of rascals in for four years, and then throwing them out and replacing them with another group of rascals for four years. From the perspective of the South, that looks very good! In a context where rascals manipulate elections and stay in power for fifteen or sixteen years, I would appreciate the chance to throw them out through peaceful elections every four years.

Thus, the complaints of the North are often the aspirations of the South. Progress in industrialised nations can be a threat to developing countries.

Ten year ago, in the euphoria of globalisation and the expansion of services and finance that followed the fall of the Berlin Wall, I advanced the idea that we were entering a fractured global order. Globalisation brings us into contact with one another, but it also strengthens profound divisions and fractures in terms of societies and income, and most importantly in our capacity to generate and utilize knowledge. Over the last ten years, the concentration of wealth and power has greatly increased both within and between societies.

There is a real risk of two civilisations emerging, with two ways of viewing and relating to the world: one based on the capacity to generate and utilize knowledge, the other passively receiving knowledge from abroad and deprived of the ability to modify it.

The world now faces the prospect of this Knowledge Divide becoming an unbridgeable abyss. We need the international community to return to the basic principles of international co-operation and introduce the idea that a minimum level of science and technological capability, including access to the Internet, is an absolute necessity for developing countries and should be the subject of international solidarity.

This can be achieved. However, contrary to the situation of 20 years ago, national governments are no longer the major players in the game of science and technology. Whether we like it or not, the private sector and the international community of scholars must be invited to the table with governments from the North and South to begin discussing an agenda for the mobilisation of a science and technology for development. United Nations with a mandate for the development of the sciences, has a special role to play in the revitalisation of international co-operation in this field.

Chapter 5

Urbanisation and Globalisation

How we handle globalisation will determine whether our cities and our civilisation will be divided and violent or user-friendly and peaceful. We cannot get a clear picture of urban life in the 21st century, especially in the poor countries of the South, unless we take into account the phenomenon of globalisation, which has already brought dramatic changes make their first appearance. So it is there too that the great upheavals of the next century will take place.

Globalisation given shape to the "Global Village". The "information era" that it ushers in compresses time and we are now living in a world speeded up as never before. Worldwide urbanisation is proceeding at a similar rate and its pace in the poor countries of the South seems terrifying. By 2025, two-thirds of humanity will be living in cities and towns, where the best opportunities in life tend to be.

Globalisation also accentuates a "new urban geography" in both North and South. Islands of rich consumers are springing up in cities amid an ocean of deprived people. More and more unemployed people, immigrants, minorities and the homeless, are pushed into cities by pressure from "market economies". As a result, all urban areas—not just those in the poor countries of the South—will have to deal with growing internal tensions. In New York, for example, the poorest 20 per cent of the population earns 15 times less than the richest 20 per cent.

Cities have always had their smart neighbourhoods and their dangerous areas. But such social and geographical segregation has changed in pace and scale because of the growth in the urban population, the increase in "illegal" migrants and rising uncertainty.

In fact, we have entered a period of historical transition, where discontinuities prevail over adjustment. Radical changes in the nature of production and jobs and the incredible concentration of capital in the hands of the financial sector and speculators weigh much heavier in our lives these days than the state's efforts to adjust and improve the market economy. Segregation in cities has been given a new lease of life whose consequences we do not know. It has reached unprecedented dimensions because of the explosive growth of urban areas.

According to one scenario, things will go badly. The growing pace of globalisation will increase uncertainty about the future. Fear and defence mechanisms will grow among people and institutions, fuelling intolerance, xenophobia and mistrust of everything new or foreign. Urban tensions will manifest themselves with increasing violence, and segregation will sharpen. Public areas will be abandoned and become dangerous no-man's lands, the wretched abode of society's rejects. Cities will lose their original function of being a crossroads for meeting and exchange.

If globalisation also continues to go hand in hand with deregulation of financial markets and an unchanged level of indebtedness of poor countries, the latter will not be able to maintain their urban infrastructures. And if on top of this there is corruption and lack of political will, challenges to the system will increase and violence will grow. Cash-strapped authorities will respond with undemocratic mafias which provide them with funds.

According to a second scenario, everything will be all right. In line with the principle that "everything the state does is public, but the state doesn't control everything that is public," a new social contract will be drawn up between the state, the market, the working population and civil society, including NGOs. Cities will develop a new quality of life by providing citizens with forum for exchange. Jobs will be created in the social sector, in the fields of the environment, education, research, culture and leisure, opening up possibilities for young people.

In the countries of the South, long-term development strategies will be drafted and urban planning practised, taking advantage of the opportunities provided by globalisation but without falling into its traps. Town planning will become part of the political process, and the state will work with the private sector, monitored by institutions of civil society. Adequate housing will be built with the help of micro-credit and controls on the price of building materials. Improved infrastructures will enable marginal areas to become part of the civilised part of the city. Democracy will come up with new ways of governing with the help of networks of involved citizens.

In a transitional scenario, action strategies should fall somewhere between these two extremes. They should include social goals so that in big urban areas a society emerges which is founded on participatory democracy and on "capitalism with a human face" or "market socialism".

But the outlook is less clear than ever. Let us hope the present transition will lead rapidly to a new revival of humanism, whose first signs we are already seeing. This would open up the road to a development which is fair, humane and peaceful.

Chapter 6

The Challenges of Globalisation

Globalisation gives rise in some quarters to fears that can lead to suspicion, protectionism, and policies that are ultimately self-destructive. Such fears cannot be allowed to frustrate the great potential of a world in which countries drawing closer together. We believe that countries can face the challenges of globalisation positively, demanding as those challenges may be.

All countries can benefit from full participation in the world's markets, including its financial markets. Protectionist pressures must be resisted and reversed, and the principles of openness and multilaterism promoted by the World Trade Organisation, the IMF, and the World Bank must be honoured. And financial market integration should be seen as a positive force: it offers access of global financial intermediation and a stimulus for more competitive and efficient domestic financial sectors; and it promotes efficiency and growth worldwide.

How encouraging it is, therefore, to see that so many developing countries in transition have been freeing up their trade and exchange systems within the framework of our structural adjustment programmes.

No country can afford to forgo the benefits of integration into global market: the alternative is marginalisation and stagnation. But all countries must take the steps to minimize the associated risks. More than ever before, countries need tightly disciplined macro-economic policies to maintain a stable environment for investors, whether domestic or foreign. And while foreign capital can be a useful—and sometimes vital complement to domestic saving, it is not a substitute for it: domestic saving remains the key to investment and sustainable growth. It is also clear that strong financial institutions are essential to avoid market disturbances at home and to secure an effective defence against external pressures. Competitive banking and financial systems that are sound, well regulated, and properly supervised are indispensable for countries to be able to expose their economies safely to the pressures that can arise in global markets.

The challenges to globalisation therefore add to the need for the developing and transition countries to press ahead with their adjustment and reform efforts. For many, this means creating conditions to attract foreign financing and use it effectively. But a growing number of countries have been facing a different problem: how to cope with large-scale capital inflows. Such inflows, especially when they are easily reversible; provide no grounds for relaxation of adjustment and reform.

They should not be used to finance domestic consumption. In many cases, they call for stronger fiscal discipline; and in some cases, exchange rates should be allowed to take part of the strain. Many developing countries and countries in transition also, of course, need to do more to deepen and widen the role of market forces and to foster more competitive market environments in order to promote transparent and efficient mechanisms for resource allocation.

Is globalisation any less demanding for the industrial countries? Not at all! It adds to the urgency of the task of taking full advantage of the current expansion to tackle the deep-rooted problems that are limiting the pace, the quality, and perhaps, the sustainability of their growth.

All has to applaud the increased efforts and commitments to reduce fiscal deficits, but in most cases underlying imbalances remain large and the pace of consolidation too slow. More must be done not only to redress present imbalances but also to meet the growing demands of the future.

Another deep-rooted problem—structural unemployment—must also be tackled sooner, rather than later. Budget laxity and high unemployment tend to feed on each other. While cyclical conditions provide the opportunity, governments must not flinch from the task of improving the functioning of labour markets. How? It is not an easy task: by reforming regulations and policies that impede employment creation and job search.

Monetary stability, macro-economic discipline, sound financial systems, and efficiently working market mechanisms are essential for all countries that embrace globalisation. But they are not sufficient for any. To fight the fears that globalisation sometimes inspires, countries need policies that promote not just economic efficiency, financial stability, and growth but also equity and high quality growth. In too many countries, the quality of growth suffers from widening distributional inequalities related partly to high unemployment but also stagnating wages of unskilled workers. And too many countries continue to suffer from poor governance, corruption and increasing crime.

Of course, economic policy can provide only part of what is needed to rid the world of these blights. But it is a vital part. To promote equity, efficiency, and sustainable growth, governments carry an inescapable responsibility for investment in human capital—through education, health care, and well-targeted social safety nets—and also for establishing and maintaining honest and effective systems of public administration, law, order and justice. If these essential services are to be affordable, there is certainly no room for unproductive expenditures—military or otherwise—and wasteful subsidies: they must bear the brunt of fiscal consolidation. So globalisation demands a lot from governments if it is to deliver its promise of stronger and high-quality growth.

REFERENCES

A.K. Sen, *Pattern of British Enterprises in India: 1854-1914,* in *Social and Economic Development,* Singh and V.B. Singh (eds), New Delhi, 1965, p. 420.

Cottrel, P.L., *British Overseas Investment in Nineteenth Century,* Macmillan, 1975.

Murphy, Rhoads, *The Outsiders: Western Experience in India and China* University of Michigan Press, 1977.

Das, Parekh and Parekh, *India Development Report* (1999), Oxford University Press.

Reich, Robert (ed), *The Power of Public Ideas,* Ballinger, Cambridge, Mass USA, 1988.

Chapter 7

High World Trade Growth Vs. Output
WTO Sees Link to Globalisation

World Trade in merchandise goods is expected to increase in volume by 8 per cent in 1995 down marginally on the very high 9½ per cent for 1994. Although the current outlook is for a further modest slowing next year, trade growth will remain above the average of the past decade.

Recent trade growth figures continue to exceed world production growth by a large margin in 1995 probably by a factor of almost three and next year close to double. This persistent pattern relates closely to the "globalisation" of the world economy; a process which, brings far-reaching benefits and which can be promoted through the further development of the multilateral trading system.

The recent growth is as follows:

- a 13 per cent rise pushed the value of world merchandise trade past the $4,000 billion mark for the first time, to $4,090 billion;
- an 8 per cent increase in the value of trade in commercial services, to $1,100 billion, after near stagnation in 1993;
- a 23 per cent increase in the dollar value of merchandise trade in the first six months of 1995 which, allowing

for the depreciation of the US dollar, is consistent with a full-year growth in trade volume of 8 per cent.

Globalisation

Over the period from (1950 when the process of trade liberalisation through the early GATT Round got under-way) to 1994, the volume of world merchandise trade increased at an annual rate of slightly more than 6 per cent and world output by close to 4 per cent. Thus, during those 45 years world merchandise trade multiplied 14 times and output 5½ times. However, the excess of trade growth over output growth varied; from an average of a mere half percentage point in the period 1974-84 to nearly 3½ percentage points in the most recent 10 years. In fact, the excess during the years since 1990 has been much higher still but it is not yet clear whether or not this represents a permanent shift to a faster rate of increase in the world's trade-to-output ratio.

To the question "will globalisation continue?" In this regard one has to observe two factors—technological change and the evolving strategies of firms and individual investors—impart a natural momentum to global integration. It is government policies which can speed-up, slow down or even reverse progress on global integration. In this context, the role of non-discrimination—in particular, through the "most-favoured-nation" (MFN) clause—is examined.

The MFN Clause

MFN was the centrepiece of a multiplicity of bilateral trade agreements reached in Europe in the second-half of the 19th century, a period marked by very low tariffs and rapidly increasing trade. In contrast, the 1920s and the 1930s saw efforts to restore liberal trade through international trade conferences rather than legally-binding commercial treaties based on MFN. The failure of these efforts contributed to the Great Depression and provided some of the roots of military confrontation in 1939. It was only after the war that negotiations established what became the GATT, a multilateral contract consisting of rules and disciplines and based firmly (Article) on MFN treatment.

The GATT system has been a post-war bulwark against a return to the trade chaos of the 1930s. In the 1990s, a disintegration of the globalised international economy on the scale of 1930s is almost unthinkable. In contrast, today "the threat that would be posed by a loss of credibility of the multilateral rules" (now represented by the WTO) would be "a fracturing of the global economy into inward-looking and potentially antagonistic trading blocs".

One can suggest two safeguards against such an eventuality:

- the examination of new ways to ensure that free-trade areas and customs unions remain outward-looking and complement rather than compete with the multilateral trading system; and
- progress in dealing, at the multilateral level, with new issues tied directly to the further evolution of the global economy. These include telecommunications, financial services, environment, competition and investment policies among others.

Progress in dealing with these and other issues at the multilateral level will have a significant impact on the future pace of global integration, both directly and through its impact on the credibility of the multilateral system in influencing the broad spectrum of national trade policies.

Chapter 8

Myths and Illusions

The tide of precarity is rising steadily, so that people who have never been poor no longer regard poverty as a distant prospect but as one so close that it could engulf them at any moment.

In 1989, the fall of the Berlin Wall was rightly welcomed because it marked the collapse of a system that provided a degree of equality but rejected freedom. Today there is a strong possibility that the system gradually spreading all over the world—a kind of neo-liberal fundamentalism—may also collapse. In its obsession with freedom, vital though freedom is, this fundamentalism disregards equality, a term which should not be regarded here in purely static and statistical terms, but as something dynamic and ethical. Equality can only be truly practised in a context of social solidarity or to borrow from the vocabulary of the French Revolution of fraternity.

On the one hand, we have a world that is immensely rich in resources, possibilities, knowledge and experience; its constituent societies are freer and more dynamic than ever. There is an extraordinary potential for everyone to live a better life. But at the same time, new and ever higher walls are being built both between peoples and between social groups within individual countries. We are experiencing a travesty of development, which is creating a world bipolarized into extremes of wealth and poverty.

The most common reactions to this disastrous situation are very often the result of two misapprehensions. The first can only be described as ideological or doctrinaire since it is not based on the facts as they can be observed. It says that since the dominant system of values and things is by definition more than satisfactory, the persistence of impoverishment is merely a temporary blip. Enough time has elapsed, however, for us to see that this is not the case, including in countries where this system has been part of the established order for more than a century. One statistic is particularly eloquent. In just over 30 years, world production has approximately doubled, but the gap has more than doubled between the income of the 20 per cent of world's people living in the richest countries and the income of the world's poorest 20 per cent, according to the United Nations Development Programme.

The second misapprehension stems from another form of blindness and illusion, namely the belief that poverty can be regarded exclusively as a moral issue, as if it had no other kind of implications for those who are not poor. Globalization is, however, a two-way process. It enable the countries of the north to export their values and their paradigms as well as their goods and capital to the countries of the south, but it also makes them much more vulnerable to the backlash of crises that afflict these countries. Even in the north, the cult of competitiveness is undermining situations once considered extremely stable. The tide of precarity is rising steadily, so that people who have never been poor no longer regard poverty as a distant prospect but as one so close that it could engulf them at any moment.

Because of inadequate socio-economic development, the extraordinary upsurge of democracy over the past 30 years remains a very fragile process, and there is a risk that the trend may be reversed. When hunger, disease and ignorance prevail, citizens' participation in decision-making becomes either non-existent or a mere charade. Democratic institutions become empty shells, representational bodies existing in form only and devoid of real significance.

Social divisions caused by economic distortions exacerbate the failures of democracy which in turn pose serious threats to civil order within countries and to peace between nations. It is high time to face these obvious facts.

Chapter 9

Renewing the State

Many view globalisation as a technology driven global order that has led to an intensification of interconnectedness among nations. This, however, is merely one fact of globalisation, and does not presuppose the ideological homogenisation or the rapid retrenchment of the welfare state that is currently underway.

The dispute over globalisation is not about the intensification of global interconnectedness. Rather, it is over the vision of the global system that globalisation projects. This vision entails a global economic system with identifiable rules of behaviour in trade, finance, taxation, investment policy, intellectual property rights, and currency convertibility, all of which are crafted along neo-liberal principles with minimal governmental regulation. This global system represents a new phase of capitalism which is "more universal, more unchallenged, more pure and more unadulterated than even before".

For many critics, globalisation is essentially an anti-democratic process that excludes the interests of a wide range of groups. But the process is not shaped by market forces alone. It is only made possible by the acquiescence if not active support of governments, especially those in advanced countries.

Governments in developing countries, meanwhile, are often said to be unable to stand up to globalisation without incurring severe costs. The government of South Africa, for example, could be punished by capital flight if it insists on implementing its agenda of social reform. The masses of South Africa, however, are likely to sustain heavier costs if the government abandons its reforming mandate. Faced with such a dilemma, governments have generally selected the side of capital for a simple reason.

The list of problems caused by globalisation is long. In low-income countries, such as those in Sub-Saharan Africa, where governments have been unable or unwilling to provide their populations with even the most basic protection from the new phase of global capitalism and structural adjustment programmes, the people's plight has been particularly severe.

Opponents of globalisation are addressing genuine problems. But it is uncertain whether they will succeed in reversing globalisation or even in mitigating its adverse impacts. To begin with, many of them are badly organised. Most of them have also rallied around specific issues instead of articulating a comprehensive counter vision. At this point, the counter vision they project appears to be a global system which is not shaped by the narrow interests of capital but which accommodates the interests of diverse social groups. This vision, however, is not yet well developed.

Further more, these opponents have yet to develop viable strategies to constrain globalisation. Some argue for weakening or even abolishing institutions such as the World Bank, the International Monetary Fund, and the World Trade Organisation, which they view as agents of globalisation, it is unclear why business interests and governments would allow this to happen. The relevance of these bodies is only likely to decline if Third World countries, especially middle-income ones, begin to reduce their dependence of them under pressure from their populations.

Yet the main problem faced by these critics is that many of them do not see the relevance of the state. A successful struggle for genuine popular democracy can liberate the state from the grip of corporate and financial interests, turning it into a critical agent for the promotion of broad social interests. Many NGOs rely instead of civil society, though this cannot substitute the state in policymaking. The struggle against globalisation is essentially a struggle for democracy; the state cannot be bypassed, but must be won.

Chapter 10

Add Value, Go Global
Can Southern Firms Break into Export Markets?

The global economy has changed beyond recognition over the last decade. Widespread economic policy reform and in particular trade liberalisation have opened up new opportunities for developing countries. In poor countries, however, the consequences of trade liberalisation are not always positive. What can the private sector do to respond better and make the most of new trading opportunities? What factors have limited the impact of economic reforms on export performance?

Why have exports from poorer countries failed to increase more rapidly following trade liberalisation? What can be done to improve performance? Research on the response of firms in the private sector to economic reform can underpin new approaches to export promotion for poorer developing countries. For a long time, protective trade policies, poorly performing state-owned industries and state controls over the private sector were blamed for poor export performance in Africa and South Asia. Now that some of these problems have been remedied, other obstacles have come to light.

The effect of economic liberalisation and adjustment on the performance of poor countries has been cause for concern. Trade liberalisation should increase incentives to export and facilitate business enterprise by encouraging private ownership through privatisation and by attracting foreign investment. Macroeconomic stability ought to boost business confidence and performance. All these factors should promote exports, offsetting job and income losses caused by the closure or reorganisation of inefficient enterprises and industries yet, although some degree of reform and stability it is without export growth that was expected.

Trade reform and macroeconomic stability may be necessary conditions for improved export performance put by them are insufficient. The obstacles to improving export performance are numerous and there is no easy policy answer. The research programme examined export performance at three levels.

- *Regional:* How trade strategies should vary with skills and natural resource endowments
- *National:* Factors influencing the export performance of manufacturing
- *Sectoral:* The performance of particular sectors of the economy.

The East Asian economies have shown that developing countries can compete successfully in global markets. For many, they provide a blueprint for economic growth applicable to many poor countries.

South Asia's comparative advantage lies in its abundant unskilled labour, while Africa's lies in its abundant natural resources. Different export promotion strategies are essential. South Asia's best prospects are in labour-intensive manufacturing: the region's low level of exports would soar over the next decade if current obstacles to trade were reduced. Africa's exports could also increase but its biggest potential in primary products that need little educated labour and abundant natural resources.

Some African countries could also be substantial exporters of manufacturers, but their actual manufactured exports in most cases now fall far short. Comparing Ghana to Mauritius—one of Africa's most successful exporters of manufactured goods differences in firm-level efficiency are apparent Mauritian firms have more capital per worker and use it more efficiently. Reducing trade barriers is not sufficient. Wages in Ghana would have to be substantially lower to offset low labour productivity. Alternatively, labour productivity will have to be drastically improved if Ghanian firms are to compete successfully in export markets with wages at current levels.

Even when companies use capital and labour efficiently, poor infrastructure is a frequent stumbling products to export markets—an acute problem in landlocked countries and equally acute for manufacturers as research on Uganda clearly shows. What huts manufacturing exporters is being hit by the high cost of transporting their output to foreign markets and of transporting the materials they need from abroad. The cost penalties resulting from geography and poor infrastructure are far greater in Uganda than from high tariffs and other import restrictions.

Southern firms can still break into export markets, however, developing—country firms do export to markets with exacting standards for product quality, reliability of delivery, and consumer safety. Two crucial aspects, however, are often overlooked:

- Non-manufacturing sectors, such as tourism and horticulture, generate significant employment and offer opportunities for supplying increasingly sophisticated products. Although manufacturing is considered more attractive, certain areas of tourism and horticulture can be equally appealing.
- New export opportunities are created as southern producers establish closer links with foreign customers. Producers of labour-intensive products such as garments,

horticulture and footwear frequently depend on large retailers and specialist international traders for designs, information about demand and technical support.

Supermarkets make key decisions about which fruits and vegetables to grow, how they should be produced and processed and which firms should be included in the business. Strategic decisions by international producers and retailers in the footwear industry have been crucial in developing new production locations such as Vietnam and Romania. Similarly, work on automotive components production in South Africa and India illustrates how global sourcing by the leading motor companies closes off some markets and opens up others. Export prospects can only be evaluated in the light of global restructuring in these industries.

Emphasising global linkages does not mean that developing countries are powerless in the face of global forces. Even in tightly-structured industries, there is scope for national policy and national strategy. Furthermore, there are important export sectors that are not structured in this way. Some tourism is dominated by large northern firms and is heavily import-dependent, but there is also enormous potential and national policy will be crucial in shaping the industry and its contribution to the economy as a whole.

For southern firms to break into export markets, certain issues must be addressed, especially in Africa. Some are recognised as important policy issues—investing in human capital and improving infrastructure for example. As one set of constraints are reduced—such as removing policy—induced distortions through trade liberalisation—another set takes precedence. In response to the integration of global markets, southern producers must join the global distribution chains to ensure markets for their exports.

These findings impose hard choices on developing countries. Should a firm allocate limited funds for investment in human capital or investment infrastructure?

Future research might contribute by quantifying relative rates of return. On another level, countries may worry about the independence and autonomy of local producers if they are to join a global chain typically donated by northern companies. Rules regulate governmental trade and investment policies but who controls the global buyers and multinational companies whose decisions have such huge impacts on developing countries?

Chapter 11

What was Wrong with Structural Adjustment

In Defence of a Much-Maligned Strategy

After decades of stranded development theories, ideologies and paradigms, "structural adjustment", with its demands for clean fiscal policy and an end to uneconomic state enterprises, political privileges, market and exchange rate intervention and corruption, entered the aid arena like a refreshing dawn after a long night of frustrating dreams. Only the "old guard" of planned economy advocates and jealous academicians who had missed the boat were able to shut their eyes to the moral and economic justification of this liberating breakthrough in international development policy spearheaded by the Bretton Woods institutions then steered by some exceptionally courageous economists.

Reaction to SAPs

As with any revolution, defeat is awaiting the pioneers at the hands of political power greed, reactionary tactics by the formerly privileged and academic envy. The principal device serving the reactionary forces as a lever of influence on the mood of the "development community" has been the identification and dramatisation of new pockets or strata of (principally urban) poverty allegedly created by structural adjustment measures, while shunning the much broader-based rise in economic activity, real incomes and sense of fair reward in the overall society, especially the rural population. That the hardship experienced by urban poor, formerly privileged under consumer price control and import subsidies to the debit depressed farm prices or maintained by grossly over-expanded public payrolls, was only laying open the camouflaged erosion of the economy and near-bankruptcy of governments and public enterprises was conveniently downplayed.

These reactionary howls were to be expected. Not that they met the entirely innocent. There had been naively sweeping, overly assuming demands by some structural adjustment missions. But an intellectually vigorous and dynamic "development community" would have coped with the ensuing opposition, strengthened the analytical and monitoring capacities and the political will to endure also rocky roads and bitter medicines on the way to a healthier base. Instead, institutional rivalry, political opportunism and emotive populism were thriving. In a way, the "development community" behaved as if it did not want its patient to become able to stand on his own feet and eventually steal its raison d'être.

Worst, the Bretton Woods institutions themselves, partly under the pressure of the emotive opposition, described above, fell to the temptation to rescue their lending volume, which was threatened by the frugality dictated to Third World public budgets under structural adjustment recipes, through hardship-easing loans. They thereby corrupted their creation in using it to reinforce their indispensability. As a consequence it soon turned out that some of the most obedient loan takers under structural adjustment terms experienced sharply rising indebtedness, exploited as a disqualifying symptom by the anti-structural adjustment camp.

Whatever the opinions on structural adjustment policies, the commitment to the principles of "good governance" has come to stay, at least on paper, as an almost standard conditionally for official development aid from

OECD donor countries. The realisation, matured in the implementation of structural adjustment programmes, that not the quantity of aid, but the quality of Third World governments determines the positive or negative course of development, may be regarded as the most valuable fruit of the decades-old policy debate in the 'development community". And the use of aid as a pressure or bribing factor towards "good governance" as foreign aid's least disputable purpose.

Out of the Limelight

Nothing, however, must be taken for granted. Achievement breeds its challenge! Structural adjustment, though in essence hardly disputable has been pushed out of the limelight and replaced by the oldest actor in the company: eradication of poverty, twinned with an equally perpetual endeavour at the macro-level: debt-forgiveness. This falling back to square one in donors' approach to the problems of the south, i.e., the call to alleviate poverty and priorities direct efforts to this end above all other developmental efforts—does it indicate a sell-out of constructive ideas in the "development community"? Has any noteworthy progress been achieved in the past by this approach?

By telling a frugally toiling but independent subsistence farmer that internationally his condition is classed as "poverty", deserving compassion and support by the world community and cancellation of his debts, one can hardly expect a sustainable improvement in his output, satisfaction, or self-respect and even less, when he realises that the help principally provides jobs, fringe benefits and self-importance to a gamut of intermediaries, at home and abroad.

What do those poverty advocates (the "Lords of poverty") really know about the resources, life managements, value systems and ambitions of those they generalize by the billions? The great variance in the conception of life situations, from different external viewpoints.

What the aid system can do for these rural populations classed as "poor"/"underprivileged"/"exploited", is press for justice, i.e., "good governance". The achievements of structural adjustment policy through, e.g. abolishing official price and exchange rate distortions, import subsidies and exploitative state agencies, has brought massive income improvement for peasant populations, i.e. the majority of LDC inhabitants, in dimensions unreachable by whatsoever direct "attack" on rural "poverty". What people want is not being benevolently treated as poor, but being justly rewarded for their work, i.e., by access to the unmanipulated market value of their output. Slackening on structural adjustment/"good governance" conditionally under the present "10 year itch" for paradigm change means foregoing much of the potential opportunities for undoing injustice and exploitation of the masses. It should be clear where priority focus should be placed in ODA policy.

Small is not Beautiful

The direct attack on "poverty", orchestrated by the Bretton Woods institutions under their freshly launched Poverty Reduction Strategy Paper (PRSP) campaign, is being rightly regarded as primarily an NGO domain, since most activities are expected to be carried out at local community level. This would require careful screening and coordinating of NGO activities and their integration via gradual expansion of their experience. But "small" is not "beautiful" for the development financing institution. Disbursement needs are pressing, calling for the new paradigm to quickly provide channels for another wave of loans to the "IDA Countries". Their problem of heavy indebtedness, which would principally exclude most of them from any new loan consideration, shall be solved with one stroke (which only the well-cushioned development bureaucracy can afford); debt relief against presentation of country PRSPs by the respective governments. NGOs are expected to play in the system especially the knowledge gap about the "poor" people's real wants and needs NGOs will naturally be tempted by such expansionary boost to their involvement (referred to sarcastically as their philanthropic empire" by an African conference participant), but this will not be conducive to quality and accountability of their performance, which ideally should be based on private sponsorship in combination with strong target-group provided self-help components.

Patience and Self-Restraint

Local knowledge and initiatives cannot be obtained under time pressure. "The grass does not grow faster by being pulled". When will the "development community" learn patience and self-restraint in the approach to LDC's capacity for constructive absorption of aid programmes accompanied by a genuine sense of ownership?

After all these deliberations, how shall development policy be shaped in order to better correspond with reality, without sinking deeper into hypocrisy and frustration?

To come back to the opening question: what was wrong with "structural adjustment"? Nothing was wrong with its intent. In fact this was very right and long overdue. Its implementation, however, lacked patience, perseverance and solid support from the development community, apart from its being corrupted as a vehicle for expansionary lending policy. If aid is meant to not be an end in itself, then structural adjustment policy needs constant reinforcement, underpinned by strict lending discipline. There should be an end to irresponsible lending and easy escape from its consequences by wholesome periodic debt relief burdened on the international tax-paying community. No ODA, either loans or grants, should be made available to governments who are not in active process of implementing "good governance" principles. A monitoring unit, reporting to the donor community on government performance in regard to its "good government"? Structural adjustment commitment, should be maintained in each and receiving country by "donor consortia" comprising all locally represented bilateral and multilateral development organisations currently extending technical, financial or material assistance to the country.

In order to accommodate the poverty focus without diluting the necessary structural adjustment orientation of ODA, a division of activity-focus between the latter and the NGO sector would seem to be advantageous.

- ODA, limited to the countries abiding to structural adjustment/"good governance" conditionally, with focus concentration on sustainable physical, social and economic infrastructure principally at national and regional level, public management training, higher education and research, consultant and senior adviser services.
- The NGO sector, principally funded by private sponsorship, united to structural adjustment conditionally (but preferably grafted on local self-help initiative), with focus-concentration on the "Third World "poor", i.e., mostly at rural community and low-income township level, for amelioration of living conditions and local resource utilisation.
- Strengthening of linkages between the NGO sector and the UN Technical Agencies to mutual benefit: NGOs in need of professional information, evaluation and advice or forum for discussion to find an actively supportive window at the agencies; the latter to maintain and develop field contact of research and policy generation, not least as a substitute for their declining project work (giving way to greater concentration on their global functions, i.e., serving as information, policy initiation, and coordination/negotiation centre on topics of global concern, such as e.g., human rights, global monetary and trade systems, tropical forest and global marine resources, global and regional health threats, international standards).

In conclusion, it may be called to mind that aid and its institutions have no claim for permanence. They are justified only as temporary functions in a phasing—out process of self-help support. Any claim for unlimited continuity would breed lasting infantilisation.

Chapter 12

For a Broader Approach to Education

In our rapidly changing world, literacy should be seen as an important evolutionary variable in every society. For the further a society progresses, the more it needs to adjust and adapt to new demands and pressures, so that literacy is lifelong necessity for all.

Literacy, in the broad sense, is the foundation for life skills, ranging from basic oral and written communication to the ability to solve scientific and social problems. Today it involves much more than the acquisition of Rs. 3. And a limited set of traditional skills. It is linked with the changing demands of life in a given socio-cultural context.

This means that local communities should be fully involved in defining the content of literacy programmes. The local dimension of literacy is externally important, not only for accommodating the real needs of learners, but also for taking into account the linguistic and cultural realities of multicultural societies. For in the end, only the learners actually decide what they need to learn.

Building Bridges Between Cultures

Most literacy specialist have accepted this broader, more dynamic and culturally sensitive stance. It marks a long overdue acknowledgement of the positive role that local language and cultures can play in removing some of the serious pedagogical and psychological hurdles often encountered by learners, it is the only way to ensure the relevance and authority of literacy work.

Any one can insist here on the importance of multilingual education. Today education is as much about learning to live together as learning to know, to do and to be. Yet we cannot live together if our possibilities of expression are limited to a single linguistic frame. This is often at the root of problems encountered in multicultural societies. Of course, inequality in all its forms is a major factor. But internal conflicts often have purely cultural causes. It is more difficult for people to forge links with each other when they cannot communicate linguistically.

Yet children learn languages easily—much more so than the adults who take the decisions. We need to take much greater advantage of this fact. Children are expected to store too much information in their "hard memory"—much of it frankly useless! Giving them language skills provides them with bridges between cultures, enabling them to grow up without the debilitating sense that other cultures are lien. It is our task to try to ensure that education at all levels, and particularly basic education, promotes multilingualism. And we must invest in such education, since to do so is to invest in peace.

It is also important to remind ourselves that literacy is not a neutral process which can be applied in all situations, all the time, regardless of social and economic realities. Such a narrow concept of literacy ignores its critical role as a tool of empowerment. One can treat adult learners as empty vessels waiting to be filled with predetermined bodies of knowledge disconnected from their social experience. Literacy must provide space of intellectual development, motivations for learning and a sense of self-esteem, if it is to be a genuine education for empowerment.

Bringing Adult Education into the Mainstream

Many individuals and families around the world are

facing unexpected changes in the pattern of their daily lives, disrupting their plans for the future. The demands on educational services are increasing dramatically, especially in countries where the state is the main provider of education for children and adults. In today's world, we cannot afford a short sighted approach which, in effect, excludes adult education from the mainstream of the education system, even after the concept of life long learning has been accepted as a framework for educational policy.

Literacy programmes must be given the priority they deserve. Lifelong learning for all requires quality adult education and literacy programmes with qualified personnel, relevant teaching programmes, appropriate post-literacy materials and decent facilities. We must ask ourselves whether we recently are prepared to make the necessary. Investments in adult education and literacy to ensure universal access to the types of programmes needed to reach the targets of education for all.

If we truly believe in lifelong learning, and if we seriously believe in redressing the balance of learning in our societies, then we should seek to develop in every country an open and more enabling system of education, breaking with past concepts of education as something which happens to people between the ages of six and twenty and which only the privileged of few were entitled to. Synergy has to be created between formal and non-formal education programmes.

A case in point is the family literacy concept. We all know that the continuing education of parents, particularly when they are illiterate or under-educated, can contribute very effectively to their children's success in school. In fact the family literacy approach is one of the must effective ways of breaking the cycle of inter-generational illiteracy. Education and training policies should include all types of learning, whether it takes place in a school, in the workplace or at home. There should be more innovation and creativity in using methods and approaches.

Chapter 13

Population Growth and Education

In contrast to the food supply challenge posed by the coming wave of population growth, the global need for teachers and classrooms will rise very slowly in the next half-century. In many countries, the school-age population is increasing much less rapidly than the overall national population. The trend illustrates that growth rates typically differ for different age strata of the population. It has also shows that declining birth rates can take decades to move through an entire population.

At the global level, for example, total population is projected to increase by 54 per cent between 2000 and 2050, but the number of children aged 5 to 14 will grow by only 6 per cent. And of the world's largest countries—accounting for 60 per cent of global population in 1995—will actually begin to see decreases in the number of children aged 5 to 14 by 2015; for several of these countries, the decline in this age group has already begun. These countries will need fewer classrooms and teachers to educate the youngest members of society (assuming they maintain current class size and student-teacher ratios).

Plenty of nations, however, still have increasing child-age populations. Where countries have not acted to stabilize population, the base of the national population pyramid continues to expand, and pressures on the educational system will be severe. In the world's 10 fastest-growing countries, for example, most of which are in Africa and the Middle East, the child-age population will increase in average 93 per cent over the next half-century. Africa as a whole will see its school-age population grow by 75 per cent through 2040.

The rapid growth in African populations is especially worrisome because of the extra burden it imposes in a region already lagging in education. Only 56 per cent of Africans south of the Sahara are literate, compared with 71 per cent for all developing countries. Few African countries have universal primary education, and secondary education reaches only 4-5 per cent of African children. Educating today's children is challenge enough; the addition of another three students for every four already there will require heroic investments in education. But the alternative is grim: without additional investments in education, today's average student-teacher ratio of 42 in Sub-Saharan Africa will reach 75 by 2040.

Many countries will be challenged to increase funding for education while ensuring that other worthy sectors also receive the support they need. With 900 million illiterate adults in the world, the case for a renewed commitment to education is easy to make. But competing for these funds are the 840 million chronically hungry and the 1.2 billion without access to a decent toilet.

The budget stresses on governments attempting to meet these basic needs would clearly be reduced with smaller populations. Mozambique and Lesotho, for example, both met the UNESCO benchmark for investment in education in 1992; 6 per cent of gross domestic product—and the two countries economies were roughly equal in size. Yet because Mozambique has many times the population of Lesotho, spending per child in Lesotho is about nine times higher than in Mozambique. For the majority of countries who do not meet the UNESCO funding standard, many of whom also fall short in providing other basic services, a decline in population pressure could help substantially to meet all of their social goals.

If national education systems begin to stress life-long learning for a rapidly changing world, as recommended by a 1998 UNESCO report on education in the twenty-first century, then extensive provision for adult education will be necessary, affecting even those countries with shrinking childage populations. Such a development means that countries that started population stabilisation programmes earliest will be in the best position to educate their entire citizenry.

Chapter 14

Corporate Ambitions in Education

Centralisation and efficiency, frequently invoking the powerful metaphor of scientific management or "Taylorism," using the stopwatch and management to discover the "one best way." These principles had been instrumental, industrialists of the time believed, in creating the industrial revolution and the wealth of powerful international companies. The quest for efficiency of those decades led to the problems we must now repair, notably the rigid and bureaucratic structure of our school systems.

Today, public schools continue to adapt new business efficiency techniques in what seems to be a constant recycling process. Scientific management, it turns out, was only the precursor to a host of ever newer management theories aimed at encouraging greater worker productivity and hence greater national wealth.

When Schools Become Levers to Attract Business Investment

These trends have echoes in the management reforms prescribed for and adopted by schools. Some seek increased efficiency through decentralised school governance while others image that outsourcing (or contracting) the management and operation of schools will lift educators' performance because incentives are lacking in secure government jobs.

All this is happening against the backdrop of economic globalisation, which inevitably creates political tensions by pitting governments against one another in competition for transnational corporate jobs and global capital. Our current era mimics the turn of the century to the extent that international capital flows and transnational production processes influence both corporation and governments. Today, technologically induced speed, growth among investors, concentration of wealth, and interconnectedness have increased the effects of this global speculation and decreased the capacity of governments to regulate business and markets. Not surprisingly, this global market ideology has been broadly recognised as a force in national education policy.

Reforming local schools becomes one of the ways that cities engage in the global competition to provide production resources to corporations. When formal schooling is seen as a key element of productive capacity, a view reinforced by the decline of manufacturing and the rise of information-based technologies, the quality of the local public school system takes on renewed importance for business leaders and local politicians alike. Today's corporate leaders have uncommon access to elect political officials and government agency heads, the wealth of large corporations to draw upon, and the ability to affect local and regional economics simply by making business decisions.

Schools are treated as engines of economic development to lure business to a particular city or state, so corporate and local political leaders cooperate in their governance and redesign. In short, school policy becomes labour policy?

This powerful combination of corporate, national and state executives is happening at the expenses of education professionals. In contrast to the turn of the century, when educators played a pivotal role in debates by emphasising the role of schools in developing citizenship, today they have been largely discredited. Selecting school leaders from outside the field has become both symptom and spur to this decrease in the educator's status. A small but influential group of school districts is choosing leaders from among the ranks of businessmen, politicians and the military, rather than educators.

All this is taking place with little evidence that recent management solutions will turn around poor schools, nor that improvements in school performance protect against declines in productivity or the business cycle. Yet there are more troubling problems with reform strategies that pit the market against government in education. One is that education is reduced to its narrowest economic purposes. According to a 1992 survey, corporate executives most want schools to emphasize "a basic understanding of math and science:" and "sound work habits such as self-discipline, timeliness and dedication to work." These are laudable goals, but reflect a narrow set of traits that employers predict their workers will need in an information economy.

The corporate model of reform pays little heed to other expectations of public schools: building just and tolerant communities, reducing distrust of one another and our shared institutions, safe guarding democratic ethics and introducing children to the cultural wisdom of the world. We are also witnessing the abandonment of many kinds of equality. Neither markets nor business ethics routinely put equality or fairness above profits. Whole groups of people will not fit the prevailing model of what it takes to be competitive in an educational market place in which competition is the guiding principle of improvement. Another disturbing trend is the anaemic citizenship that economic justifications for schooling envision. Increasing the emphasis on individualism is likely to exacerbate a pattern of civic disengagement many already find disturbing in its scale and scope.

A Balancing Act to Reach a Healthy Equilibrium

We need a contemporary counter-movement to restore a healthy equilibrium of goals for our public schools. This movement would be grounded in a very different educational critique that rejects the metaphor of market (or management) failure and instead tackles the problems in our schools as symptoms of a widespread civic breakdown. The solutions to school failure would then hinge on common concerns, rather than rigorous individual competition and accountability. In addition to academic criteria parents and reformers would craft student performance measures that reward active citizenship, tolerant and respectful behaviour, and cultural knowledge in the arts, history and languages. This reform movement, seeking equity and tolerance, would revitalize democratic institutions and not merely aim for more efficient production.

Chapter 15

Private Education
The Poor's Best Chance?

Across the developing world, private schools and education companies are not only flourishing, but reaching the poor. India is a case in point. A common assumption about the private sector in education is that it caters only to the elite, and that its promotion only serves to exacerbate inequality. On the contrary recent research points in the opposite direction. If we want to help some of the most disadvantages groups in society, then encouraging deeper private sector involvements is likely to be the best way forward.

Several developments are underway in India, all of which involve the private education sector meeting the needs of the poor in distinct ways. But India is not unique in this respect—similar phenomena are happening all over the developing world.

As a point of departure, how do government schools serve the poor? Usefully, the government sponsored Public Report on Basic Education in India (PROBE) from 1999 paints a very bleak picture of the "malfunctioning" of government schools for the poor. When researchers called unannounced on their random sample of schools, only 53 per cent had any "teaching activity' going on. In 33 per cent, the head teacher was absent. Alarmingly, the team noted that the deterioration of teaching standards was not to do with disempowered teachers, but instead could be ascribed to "plain negligence." They noted "several cases of irresponsible teachers keeping a school closed....for months at a time," many cases of drunk teachers, and head teachers who asked children to do domestic chores. Significantly, the low level of teaching activity occurred even in those schools with relative good infrastructure, teaching aids and pupil-teacher ratios.

But is there any alternative to these schools? Surely no-one else can do better than government given the resources available? As it happens, the PROBE report were serving the poor and conceded—rather reluctantly—such problems were not found in these schools. In the great majority of private schools—again visited unannounced and at random—there was feverish classroom activity. Most parents would prefer to send their children to private schools if they could afford them. Private schools, they said, were successful because they were more accountable: "the teachers are accountable to the manager (who can fire them), and, through him or her, to the parents (who can withdraw their children)." Such accountability was not present in the government schools, and "this contrast is perceived with crystal clarity by the vast majority of parents".

The Way Forward: Loosen Regulations and Set up Voucher Schemes

To many readers, the existence of these private schools for the poor will come as a surprise. It was to me too, until I had the privilege of conducting field work for the International Finance Corporation (the private finance arm of the World Bank) on a group of such schools operating under the banner of the Federation of Private Schools' management based in Hyderabad, the federation has 500 private schools (from kindergarten to grade ten) serving poor communities in slums and villages. I was impressed by both the entrepreneurial spirit within these schools—they were run on commercial principles, not dependent on hand-outs from state or philanthropy—but also by the spirit of dedication within the schools for the poor communities served: not for nothing were the leaders of the schools known as "social workers". But these schools suffer under restrictive and inappropriate regulations. One example will suffice: to be recognised a school must deposit upto 50,000 rupees (about $1.200) in a stipulated bank account, of which neither the capital nor the interest can be touched. Given that the fees charged in these schools ranged from 25 (60 cents) to Rs. 150 per month (about $3.50) with most of the schools grouped near the lower end of the range, such sums are completely prohibitive.

Fees of around $10 per year are not affordable by everyone, but they are to a large number of poor families. Furthermore, the great majority of the schools offer a significant number of free places—up to 20 per cent—for the poorest students, allocated on the basis of claims of need checked informally in the community.

All of this suggests that if one is interested in serving the needs of the poor in India, then trying to reform the totally inadequate, cumbersome and unaccountable government system is unlikely to be the best way. Instead, reform the regulatory environment to make it suitable for the flourishing of private schools for the poor, help build private financing schemes using overseas and indigenous philanthropy, and encourage public voucher schemes so that parents can use their allowance of funding where they see the schools are performing well, rather than wasting them in unresponsive state schools.

Private education in developing countries isn't just about the poor, of course, and there are many exciting examples of big education businesses. But these too have implications for the ways in which the private sector can reach the least advantaged One Indian company which embodies much of the excite the National Institute for Information Technology (NIIT). With its competitor, Aptech, it shares just over 70 per cent of the information technology education and training market in India estimated at roughly Rs. 1.1 billion ($24 million). NIIT has 40 wholly owned centres in the metropolitan areas, and about 1,000 franchised centres across India. It also has a global reach, with centres in the US, Asian Pacific, Europe, Japan, Central Asia and Africa. A key aspect of NIIT's educational philosophy is that there is a need to harness research to improve the efficiency of learning and to raise educational standards.

Because of its success in developing innovative and cost-effective IT education and training, NIIT has attracted the attention of several state governments. First off the mark was Tamil Nadu, which wanted to bring a computer curriculum to all of its high schools. Significantly, although allocating about $22 million over five years to this endeavour, it didn't hand the funds over to government schools, perhaps in light of the PROBE report's lessons. Instead, it developed a model to contract out the service to private companies, which provide the software and hardware, while the government supplies electricity and the classroom. For the first round of the Tamil Nadu process, 43 contracts were awarded for 666 schools, with NIIT allotted 371 schools. Many of the classrooms have become NIIT centre, open to school children and teachers I daytime, then used by the franchise-holder in the evenings. The contracting out of curriculum areas such as this represents an important step forward in relationships between the public and private sectors, and provides an interesting model worth watching and emulating.

Most recently, NIIT has focused on reaching largely illiterate and unschooled children through the Internet. Within weeks of having set up an "Internet kiosk" in a slum area, the institute's researchers found that without any instruction, children could achieve a remarkable level of computer literacy. NIIT is exploring ways to roll out the idea commercially, harnessing the power of the private sector to reach the poorest through modern technology.

These initiatives all find echoes in other developing countries. In each case, the private, not the public sector, is most responsive to the needs of the poor, and is bringing innovation, efficiency and educational quality to the lives of the most disadvantaged. The private sector has the potential to promote greater equity and to influence education policy, provided it is encouraged and viewed as a partner, not a threat to governments, whether in the developing or the developed world.

Chapter 16

Will Education Go to Market?

The World Trade Organisation has launched processes that could open up to competition the expanding and highly protected world market in education. What issues are at stake? Most of us see education as first and foremost a public service which is responsible for providing young people with instruction. For investors looking for somewhere to put their money it is also an annual budget of $1,000 billion worldwide, a sector employing 50 million people, and above all a billion potential customers in the form of students.

The decision to extend services the liberalisation of international trade which previously applied to commodities was taken in 1994. The General Agreement on Trade in Services (GATS) which was signed in April of that year included education on the list of services to be liberalised. To say outside the scope of this agreement a country's education system must be completely financed and administered by the state, which is no longer the case anywhere. However, each country can still decide freely what commitments it wants to make, and especially which educational sectors it wants to expose to market forces. The New Zealand government, for example, has decided to open up to outside competition the whole private education sector, from primary to university level.

So far, New Zealand is an exception, but that situation is likely to change. Part 4 of the GATS agreement ("Progressive liberalisation") requires that fresh negotiations should be held by the end of 2000 at the latest, and should be directed to "the elimination of the adverse effects on trade in services of measures as a means of providing effective market access". At the Geneva headquarters of the World Trade Organisation (WTO), far from the headlines and the demonstrators, work still goes on. But independently of the WTO and national policies, a number of factors are driving educational systems towards "communication".

Pressures for Change

First, education is a rapidly-growing sector in which governments are finding it harder and harder to satisfy demand, above all in higher education. Between 1985 and 1992, the number of students in higher education rose about 26 per cent—from 58.6 to 73.7 million. Meanwhile, public spending on education has tended to stagnate over the past 15 years (5-6 per cent of GDP in rich countries and 4 per cent elsewhere).

In view of this dearth of public spending, parents and students are increasingly looking to private education for a solution. In the United States, every episode of violence in a state school and every scandal that rocks official school systems gives a boost to "home schooling", where children no longer attend school and are taught at home.

Traditional public education is also coming in for strong criticism. Employers complain it is not geared to their needs and is not flexible enough. Under pressure from economic interests, a process of "deregulating" education system has begun. The growing independence of schools is encouraging them to look for alternative sources of funding, ranging from sponsorship to full management by private companies and including many kinds of partnerships between schools and firms. The time for out-of-school education has come... the liberalisation of the educational process thereby made possible will lead to control by education service providers who are more innovative than the traditional structures.

The development and spread of information and communication technologies on a massive scale make possible the development of paid distance learning, using multimedia and the Internet for tutorials, examinations, etc.

Secondary and primary education are also affected. More and more paying Internet sites bill themselves as alternatives to state schools or traditional private schools. The computer screen takes over from the teacher, for a fee of around $2,250 a year.

The WTO secretariat set up a working group in 1998 to look at prospectus for more liberalised education. Its report pointed to the rapid growth of distance learning and noted the increasing number of partnerships between educational institutions and private firms.

Education for Export

Some 350 US experts on international trade in services, including 170 businessmen and women, gathered at the US Commerce Department in Washington on October 16, 1998 to draw up recommendations for the US negotiators at the WTO. The purpose of the meeting, called Services 2000, was to look at how the US government should continue to support the efforts of American business to take competitive advantage in foreign markets. The US currently controls about 16 per cent of the world market in services. Its services exports have more than doubled in the past 10 years and now cover 42 per cent of the non-services trade deficit.

The United States is also the world's leading exporter of educational services, and a working group at the Services 2000 conference paid special attention to this sector. It concluded that the sector "needs the same degree of transparency, transferability and interchangeability, mutual recognition, and freedom from undue regulation or restraints and barriers that the United States acknowledges on behalf of other service industries". The report said that three points should be at the centre of WTO negotiations about education.

Firstly, there should be a free flow of electronic information and means of communication, nationally and internationally. Secondly, the negotiators should tackle "barriers and other restrictions that limit or prevent the provision of educational and training services across countries and internationally." They were also to deal with obstacles to the transferability of degree and diplomas.

Fighting for Market Share

The US demands are backed by most countries of the APEC (Asia-Pacific Economic Cooperation) zone. In a note in October 1999, the Australian delegation to the WTO said it would be "encouraging all members to make expanded commitments in all sectors, even the ones that have proved difficult in both regional and multilateral services negotiations", particularly education.

South Korea took a similar position. At a meeting of Ministers of Human Resources from APEC Countries that it hosted in September 1997, the Seoul government put out a memorandum which clearly stated its vision of education as a tool of economic competition.

"The emphasis on education for itself or on education for good members of a community without a large emphasis on preparation for future work is no longer appropriate. Such a view of education and work cannot be justified in a world where economic development is emphasised.

"At present, in many economies, the education system do not sufficiently reflect labour market conditions. Their inflexible and inefficient education systems could not meet the new economic environmental challenges." So education should be made more "flexible", i.e. be deregulated and liberalised. In particular, "School systems should be established to allow all students to study what they are interested in" and "employers, with school educators, should share the role of educating students".

Some think resistance to liberalizing education will come from Europe, especially France. "The future WTO negotiations cannot call in question France's tradition of public service in the field of education and health", stressed a report on the WTO.

Chapter 17

Wanted
An New Deal for the Universities

Higher education must meet new demands in order to turn out well-trained professionals instead of unemployed graduate. We are living through a period of profound historical change, marked by an ongoing knowledge revolution. Society is changing far more quickly than the structures it has created and the quickly than the structures it has created and the universities are lagging behind these changes. They, and the educational system in general, continue to teach the use of static processes, forecasting models based on historical experience and the memorizing of solutions to already solved problems.

Higher education systems in both North and South are in crisis, both quantitatively and qualitatively. Naturally the developing countries are the hardest hit, both in terms of available resources and levels of student enrollment.

Is the crisis due to a shortage of funds alone? Does the fact that the countries of the North invest ten times more per student than those of the South mean that graduates from the former are ten times better trained? Common sense says yes. But in most cases the answer is no. Generally speaking, university education has failings all over the world, in some cases because it is an offspring of a wasteful society, indifferent to the resources with which that society provides them.

The Missing Link between Education and the World of Work

In the United States, for example, many teachers and researches come from developing societies which should theoretically have given them a less sound training than that provided by the immense academic and financial resources of the United States system. But this is not the case: they compete professionally and scientifically, with no major problems. In many areas the results of university training are comparable.

Professionals move around because they need jobs and want to work in the best possible working conditions. There are, for example, almost 30,000 African Ph.Ds working in Europe and North America, and thousands of Latin American and Asian professionals working in the United States. By the beginning of the 1990s about a million professionals had emigrated to the developed countries over the previous three decades, and the figure has increased considerably in the last five years. While the number of opportunities and access to them are uneven, there is little difference between North and South as regards quality; nor is the availability of funding the only basis for improving the system.

The problem is that post-secondary training today is diploma-driven. It is based on rigid study programmes and is changing at a rate which takes little or no account of the speed of knowledge accumulation. This is despite the fact that today's graduate professional needs to have followed a flexible curriculum and must be a problem solver, extremely adaptable to new processes and technologies, generously endowed with creativity and firmly inclined towards lifelong learning, as is clear from the studies on skilled labour done by industrialized countries and from numerous OECD studies.

A recent study of the relationship between higher education and the labour market observes that there appears to be no connexion between the increase in professionals' level of knowledge and changes on the labour market. Although the market undoubtedly demands basic skills and knowledge, it is attaching increasing importance to the emotional and psychological attitudes of future employees.

Although post-secondary education is clearly associated with higher personal incomes, lower unemployment and greater opportunities to climb the social ladder, unemployment rates for people with higher education qualifications continue to be high in both North and South. Graduates unemployment in Europe, for example, varies between 1.4 per cent and 16.6 per cent depending on the country. What's more, many graduates are working in jobs outside their field of training. The increase in graduate unemployment in the developing countries is largely due to the drastic fall in demand from the major employer of graduates—the state—as a result of international competition and new political and economic approaches. The private sector is in no position to absorb the supply of surplus graduates. World Bank studies carried out in Asia, the Middle East, North Africa and certain Latin American countries show that graduate employment is increasing.

All the same, higher education cannot be held wholly responsible for graduate unemployment nor for the correlation that should exist between training, study programmes and demand for labour. It is often said that higher education is failing to provide training in the activities required by the market, but the market is often incapable of adequately anticipating the type of professionals it is going to need.

A survey conducted in Florida (USA) among multinationals in the high-tech and services sectors revealed companies that were unable to identify the professional qualities that would be required within ten years and, in many cases, within five years. This is not surprising, in view of the spectacular rise of the Internet between 1994 and 1998 which caught many hardware and software firms unawares. It is in information technology that redundancies and high unemployment levels are occurring, because systems are constantly changing and because of strategic mergers between the major companies.

Another example of the difficulty of making reliable predictions concerns those made by the European Community and the US Government regarding the type of jobs that would be needed at the beginning of the new century. These predictions were inaccurate: what had been forecast to occur after 2001 actually came about in the late 1980s and early 1990s.

It can be said, however, that professional training over the come years will focus on areas such as high-tech electronics, information technology, aqua-culture, agro-energy, biotechnology and energy physics. Jobs in information and communication systems will require new qualifications which will have to be continually updated. The service sector will experience spectacular growth in the field of leisure and recreation because of the reduction in working hours. New professions in the human sciences such as "ludicadology", incorporating psychology, pedagogy, information science and the technology of education, play and creativity programmes, will replace the old single-discipline approach.

In short, the great occupational change looming ahead will call for increased interdisciplinary, revitalisation of the disciplines related to thick and aesthetics and sweeping changes in the attitudes of teachers and students: for the professional of the future, education will be a lifelong process, and education and work will go hand in hand.

The great challenge will thus be to create a stable relationship between higher education and society through strategic alliances with the production system designed to promote participation by all sectors of the economy in the university's basic and applied research programmes and by production-sector specialists in university teaching.

The problems of the university are also those of society, and so are the responsibilities. This rises the question of the university's specific culture, especially the teacher-student relationship. Planning is currently based above all on the teaching staff, which is more corporatist than academic. Physical spaces, salary scales, curricula, structures and timetables are more closely geared to the needs of the teacher than of teaching. This is the case all over the world.

More serious still, this teacher-centred culture is giving way to one that is even more dangerous for the survival of university education: an administration-centred culture. This would mean an education system dominated by bureaucrats and the kind of management structures which would place an institution whose function is to produce and disseminate knowledge on the same footing as a detergent factory or a multinational travel agency.

But no strategy for change can work unless higher education adapts to the challenge of the knowledge explosion. It is vital that course content should be geared to what learners "must know" and not to what teachers "know" or "think they know". This will force teachers into a permanent renal of theories, techniques and processes, keeping up with knowledge produced both inside and outside the university. Higher education is evolving towards a model in which lecturers and students will be permanent learners and where curricula will be drawn up on the basis of innovation, fresh knowledge and the latest teaching and learning technologies. Above all the university must teach people to think to use common sense and to give free rein to the creative imagination.

Chapter 18

Wiring up the Ivory Towers

Prestigious universities are forging alliances to conquer a share of the e-learning market and stand up to virtual competitors. Just like airline companies, universities around the world are forming partnerships and consortia in response to the pressures of globalisation. The World Education Market held in Vancouver was a timely sign: the fair, expressly organised to foster relations between universities, training providers, software companies and representatives from nations with large education needs attracted participants from over 60 countries.

This race to "partner up" is fuelled by a number of factors. In most industrialised countries, government funding for higher education has decreased, forcing institutions to look for new markets either to subsidize campus programmes or just to remain viable. There is a growing need for lifelong learning as "jobs for life" vanish and the information society drastically reduces the shelf-life of almost any educational qualification. Technological developments, increasingly necessary for learners in all fields to master, offer ever more innovative tools for supporting e-learning.

For business, online learning is "the" new market opportunity with the need for retraining and professional updating predicted to increase an $11.5 billion industry by 2003. Business is better able to develop and maintain the technological infrastructure necessary to run large online systems and everyone, including the universities, recognizes that it takes robust telecommunications technology to deliver education and training on the scale demanded.

A host of companies has sprung up to help universities shape and package courses for online presentation, while network providers are jockeying for position to deliver online education.

The United States is the undisputed leader in the field, prompting governments in the UK, Canada and Australia to commission being eroded by US ventures turned global Canada and the UK are in the early stages of setting up their own virtual universities. But what has become clear is that the conservative and labyrinthine decision-making processes which characterize most university procedures are being jolted by a race to get a share of the lifelong learning market.

So far, the most common approach for universities to break into the e-learning universe has been to develop courses specifically for a corporate partner or to form alliances among themselves. Universities 21, a company incorporated in the UK is a network of 18 leading universities in ten countries.

Very often, prestigious universities has stayed clear of going fully online, seeing a danger to their brand name. Many are limiting their offerings to continuing education programmes and/or non-degree courses, and more often than not, they are aiming at the corporate market. One Company UNext.com, has partnered with first-class institutions such as the University of Columbia (US) and the London School of Economics to create online courses marketed under the name Cardean University. Their target: the Fortune 500 companies as well as individual adults. They've managed to attract noble laureates to design courses and the universities have formed spin-off for-profit companies specifically to develop online programmes. This facilities the commercialisation of software and other products, and is a way to take a commercial approach to continuing and professional studies without compromising the univesity's standing.

Then there are the free-standing for profit virtual universities which are arousing the ire of institutions that have prided themselves on a long history of public service. The most quoted examplar is Phoenix University, the largest private outfit in the US Now owned by the Apollo Group, it operates the country's largest online programme with 12,200 students. The university tracks students progress and contacts those who don't submit assignments on time or fail to enrol in subsequent courses. Many critics question Phoenix's blatant commercialisation, but few doubt the university's impact on continuing professional development provision.

Although e-learning is in its infancy, its impact can already by gauged. New providers are coming on the market all the time and the trend is accelerating to the point of upsetting universities virtual monopoly in educational accreditation. An Information Technology training course offered or accredited by Microsoft has undoubtedly become more valuable than a Bachelor of Science from a renowned university.

The more consumerist the approach of the education provider, the more what is taught is influenced by demand. MBAs dominate e-learning provision and IT courses are a close second. While the new consumer/learner demands flexibility, choice and just-in-time learning opportunities, suppliers will inevitably arise who are focused on meeting the demand at the expense of quality and value. And is the consumer really the best judge of what course material to choose? Education is a more complex "product" than toothpaste or washing powder. A totally consumer driven education market is unlikely to be in society's best interest in the long term. The commercialisation of education usually goes hand-in-hand with desegregation: course design, delivery, tutoring assessment and accreditation may be carried out by different organisations. Students might study courses or modules from different universities or providers and then put themselves forward for examination and accreditation by yet another institution. While most academics loathe marking assignments, they regard this scenario with horror, and blame commercialisation for the demise of the 'community of scholars' concept of a university. The death of the 'course' has also been predicted, with learners—especially corporate and on-the job learners—demanding short study modules. What then happens to the ability to get an overview of a field when learning consists of the students selecting a whole series of unconnected learning "bites"? Learners will be "zapping" between short sequences or presentations much as they do between television channels.

But while some faculty view e-learning with alarm, technology-based learning is where most of the pedagogical innovation is taking place in universities. Multimedia learning resources and interactive simulations are being developed for the web. Collaborative learning activities, new forms of online assessment and small group teaching technologies are making online courses more stimulating, interactive and attractive than many face-to-face taught courses.

Despite "doom and gloom scenarios", most moderate observers of the scene see a continued future for the campus university, especially at the undergraduate level, while e-learning will above all cater to adult professional and independent learners. Some commercialisation of education is good if it fosters innovation, concern for quality and responsiveness to consumer demands. But if some is good, more is not necessarily better! Not in education at least.

Chapter 19

Shaking the Ivory Tower

Universities have changed radically to keep pace with modern life. No where are they heading in this high-speed age? In the past half century higher education has been transformed from a privilege conferred on social and political elites to a mass activity available to whole populations. This process began in the United States in the 1940s and 1950s, spread to most of Western Europe and many other developed countries during the 1960s and 1970s and in the past two decades has become a global phenomenon. In the next half century it will accelerate, leading perhaps to the replacement of "higher education" (still an elite-ish category despite its expansion) by extended systems of "lifelong learning".

The key to this transformation has been the expansion of secondary education. For example, in all but two countries of the OECD (Organisation for Economic Cooperation and Development) at least two thirds of young people now complete upper secondary education, and so are eligible to enter higher education. The result has been a dramatic increase in enrollment rates in higher education. In Chile the total number of students has grown from 131,000 in 1978 to 235,000 in 1988 and to 343,000 in the mid 1990s. Even in the United States, the pioneer of mass-access higher education where very high secondary education completion rates had already been achieved before 1970, the student population has continued to grow, from 11 million in 1978 to 13 million in 1988 and now to more than 14 million.

The forces have driven up completion rates in upper secondary education and enrollment rates in higher education. The first has been democratisation. As late as 1945 high levels of social, and hence educational, inequality persisted even in democratic countries, and much of the world remained in the grip of colonial and totalitarian powers. In North America, Western Europe and Australasia democratisation typically took the form of the development of "welfare states" in which there was an increase in public expenditure on education, housing, health and social security that was sustained over more than three decades after the end of the Second World War.

More recently, as renewed emphasis has been placed on the market even in social policy, the rise of consumerism has continued to fuel demands for increased higher education opportunities. The older idea of education as a civil entitlement has been compounded by newer notions of free access to the education marketplace. Far from arresting the advance to mass higher education, consumerism has accelerated it in most developed countries. As traditional forms of social differentiation based on class, gender and ethnic origin have been eroded by democratisation and by market forces, new forms based on educational certification have become more important. In many developed countries the middle class and the "graduate class" have tended to coalesce.

In much of Asia and Africa democratisation took the form of decolonisation. In newly independent countries the energy originally generated in liberation struggles against the colonial powers was directed into a wider struggle to create fairer and more equal successor societies. Education was central to this struggle. The result has been a rapid increase in higher education enrollment, for example, in

Tunisia from barely 2,000 students at the time of independence to more than 100,000 today. That process continues.

However, the relationship between democratisation and the development of higher education has been less straightforward in developing countries. Despite very rapid rates of expansion the "metropolitan" influences of the former colonial powers have lingered more stubbornly in higher education than at other levels of education. This is partly due to the continued influence of associations between universities in the British Commonwealth as well as those between francophone universities.

Partly because of these lingering "metropolitan" models and partly because levels of participation are still lower than in developed countries, many African or Asian universities have remained more elite institutions than higher education institutions in North America and Europe. Also, as economic conditions have worsened in some developing countries, the competition between primary and higher education sharpened in the post-independence years as both were seen as equally important priorities. This competition was often reinforced by the intervention of the World Bank.

The second force driving up higher education enrollments has been the changing nature of the labour market. Traditional occupations have become comparatively less significant, while new service occupations, which often require graduate-level skills, have become more important.

Skill requirements have been become more sophisticated. Jobs once done by unskilled or semi-skilled workers are now undertaken by technicians; and those which as recently as the 1980s were taken by technicians are now likely to be filled by graduates. The capital invested for every worker has more than doubled in the past 20 years. Even in occupations where there is less evidence that skills contents have changed significantly, university graduates are now employed in much larger numbers, partly to enhance the social status of these occupations and partly to compete in a graduate-dominated labour market. Health care is a good example. Once doctors were the only graduates; today, many para-medical workers are also trained in higher education.

The second form taken by the economic driver has been the growing conviction that national success now depends on economic competitiveness which, in the context of a knowledge-based economy, depends in turn on an adequate supply of human capital. Knowledge is now seen as the key economic resource.

This analysis my be exaggerated; raw materials are still very important in national economies and the global economy. But it has become pervasive—and persuasive. The naïve and linear theories of human capital popular a generation ago which postulated a direct link between investment in education and economic growth may have been challenged; some forms of higher education are now as likely to be labelled consumption as investment goods. Nevertheless, the discourse of the "Knowledge Society" has become even more powerful.

The impact of democratisation and economic competitiveness on higher education has been immense. First, the expansion of student numbers has made the cost of higher education a significant element within national budgets for the first time. A number of important consequences has flowed from this—the opportunity, and incentive, to compare the value of investing in different levels of education; increasing demands that universities are run as efficiently as possible (compromising their traditional autonomy from the state—and the market); lower unit costs as budgets have been trimmed (which may have undermined higher education's claim to represent academic excellence). Second, higher education systems have emerged that embrace not only traditional universities but also non-university institutions. Two effects have been produced. One is that the ethos of the traditional university has been eroded; it no longer stands in glorious isolation. The other is that institutional differentiation has been encouraged, whether through active state planning or in response to markets for teaching and research.

The prospects for the next half century are for an acceleration of both drivers, to include access to higher education among the basic entitlements enjoyed by citizens in democratic societies; and to "put knowledge to work" in order to generate wealth and to improve the quality of life. The prospects for higher education during the same period are also relatively easy to predict increased efficiency (which is likely to include growing pressure to make students contribute more to the cost of their higher education); greater accountability, although more probably in a "market" than a "planning" mode as even the state redefines its role as the purchaser of higher education services, more differentiation, both between and within higher education institutions, as they struggle to identify markets niches; and possibly growing demands that higher education become more relevant as instrumental considerations triumph over idealistic ones.

However, the future may be more complex than the past. In the second half of the 20th century the encounter between higher education and society has been comparatively straightforward. Although dynamic, society has presented a familiar enough face. It was characterized by a combination of bureaucratic rationality and secular (and liberal) individualism. The beneficence of science and technology was uncontested. The dominant economic model was of large scale industry, or analogous organisations in the corporate and public sectors. Although rapidly evolving, concepts and categories like "career" and "profession" remained valid. Higher education too was familiar enough. Despite the great expansion of student numbers and its adoption of novel roles, the university continued to be recognizable as such. Other types of higher education institution have been deeply influenced by university values and practices.

In the first half of the 21st century both society and higher education may become problematical and so contested categories. Some of these uncertainties are already emerging. Once firm demarcations between public and private domains, whether in terms of the balance between the state and the market or between social "spaces" and individual desires; between producers and users; between investment and consumption; between work and leisure are becoming increasingly fuzzsy in the emerging post-industrials society. Wealth is being generated by the production of "symbolic" as well as—or more than—material goods. Value is created by design, sales, marketing, service rather than by primary production. Institutions of all kinds, civic and corporate, are being challenged by the rise of adaptable and flexible organisations, made possible by advances in communications and information technology.

The force of globalisation amounts to much more than round—the clock-round—the world financial markets or an emerging international division of labour; it is not only undermining nation states but also reconfiguring time and space to produce global intimacies, again with the help of the information revolution. Social identities are no longer moulded by the "givens" of religion, class and gender, or by positions within the occupational structure, as they have been since the advent of the industrial revolution in Europe two centuries ago. Instead they are being subsumed by a process of individualisation in which life-styles rather than life-chances predominant.

Higher education will have not only to continue to satisfy the predictable demands for democratic entitlement and socio-economic utility with which it is familiar, but also to cope with the consequences of these new uncertainties. These may include; new curricula that emphasis style and images at the expense of skills and information; recategorisation of higher education as a playful, even selfish, activity; a tighter link between experience of higher education and social esteem; submergence of the universal, but also particular, values characteristic of the traditional university by anomic globalisation; threats to the scientific tradition and methods, from the "risk society", from subjectivisation and from demands that other knowledge traditions are accorded equal respect.

The universities of the 21st century, therefore, may have to face two ways. They will have to continue to pay attention to the democratisation and the "knowledge society" agendas, which are likely both to be subsumed in a larger "lifelong learning" agenda. Their ability to sustain current levels of public funding and to satisfy their student-customers will depend on their success in this respect. It will not be easy. There is a danger that the essence of higher education will be lost if it succumbs to unconstrained populism. If this happens, the "quality" of the university will disappear and with it perhaps its distinctiveness and so its utility and marketability. Similarly in the knowledge society of the future the university will face new rivals because all organisations will need to become "learning organisations". These rivals strength will be increased if the superiority of universal science is successfully challenged.

But universities will also have to address the new agendas or the "death" of work (land graduate careers?), of new social movements (and the erosion of individual enlightenment, of globalisation and virtualisation (and the undermining of academic community?); of "alternative" knowledge traditions and, perhaps even, anti-cognitive values with the undermining of "objective" science and further erosion of a common intellectual culture.

Chapter 20

Promotion of Higher Education in Research

The central role of universities in the development of skills and knowledge as an absolute prerequisite for national development is undisputed. Higher education institutions have the responsibility for training a country's high level professional, technical and managerial personnel, they are to generate new knowledge through research and advanced scientific training, and they serve as agents in the transfer, adaptation and dissemination of knowledge. Higher education institutions also play an important role in contributing to the social cohesiveness of a nation and as a forum for constructive debates on development.

In a world economy which is heavily science-based and technology-driven higher education institutions, and particularly universities, have to provide such a competence which is indispensable for building a country's endogenous capacity for problem identification and problem solution through education combined with research. In India, however, universities have so far not been able to fulfill these roles, partly because the multiplicity of their missions is hardly compatible. Many critics of the universities in India consider them to be institutions of learning and research separated from the main stream of the economic and social needs of the population which they are supposed to serve. Most of them have not managed to reconcile the missions of providing country-oriented training and research and of being part of a wider international scientific community. Higher education institutions in many countries all over the world are confronted with a large scale and mostly uncontrolled expansion of the higher education sector and the concomitant growth expenditure against a background of dwindling financial resources to support such expansion. As a result of this expansion the quality of teaching and research has declined due to overcrowding, inadequate staffing, poor physical facilities and equipment. In addition universities often show a poor capacity for management and administration. This results in a low internal efficiency which amongst others is responsible for a rising graduate under or unemployment.

These deficiencies and a lack of national resources produce dependence on external sources particularly for research development. The low capacity for planning and management makes it difficult to properly employ external sources so that there may be pockets of good quality research in one field unrelated to neighbouring areas and not forming part of an endogenous research tradition.

Measures to be Taken

The measures may be aimed specifically at increasing the efficiency of the system of higher education or of individual institutions by improving development relevance, quality and performance. More specifically are:

- to optimise and diversify the structure in line with the country's development requirements;
- to improve the capacity for efficient planning and administration;
- to diversify funding sources, with the aim of relieving the state budget;
- to improve access for talented students from all segments of society, giving special attention to the proportion of women studying.

At the level of individual institutions of higher education the aim should be improve:

- education and training performance in the academic-scientific and vocational field;
- research and development capacities, especially in applied fields;
- the capacities to provide constancy and services to contractors in state, business and industry, and society.

In order to achieve these objectives, it is necessary:

- to train the academic, administrative and technical staff;
- to improve the infrastructure including central facilities and means of communications; and
- to increase efficiency by improving organisation.

The concept stresses the importance of measures designed to increase the efficiency of higher education in general through the strengthening of management capacities both at the system and at the institutions levels. This extends, *inter alia,* to the diversification of institutions of higher education in line with development needs, diversification in terms of funding (including cost-sharing through fees) diversification in terms of study courses and practice-oriented training offered. Academic training at different levels for technical and executive staff.

New Areas of Promotion

The promotion of higher education institutions and subjects considered relevant for development (agriculture, natural sciences, engineering, medicine), the revised concept has to include areas such as the protection of the environment and resources, education, family planning and population policy.

In the wake of the political and economic reorientation taking place in many countries subjects like economics, law and social sciences are increasing in importance.

Prospects

Each country needs capacities which can produce the necessary analytical competence and research for generating information needed for designing and monitoring its development path. Institutions of higher education are essential in providing this competence. The responsibility for advanced education and the production of ideas and information should not be left to external donors. This may entail the concentration of resources, both internal and external, on one or only a few institutions of a country.

Chapter 21

Heating up Environmental Education and Communication

Worldwide environmental issues ranging from the hazardous waste in your backyard to ozone depletion far away in the atmosphere can threaten our planet and compromise our quality of life. The positive and negative effects of environmental interactions are just beginning to be better understood and addressed. Within this context, environmental education and communication have a remarkable opportunity to accelerate understanding and to mobilise national and community participation in change.

Communication because it is the exchange of information. In social programmes, its effectiveness depends on assessing audience needs and taking into account the social, cultural and economic aspects of a problem as well as the quality of education messages and materials.

Education because it involves learning—learning how to think about an issue and its solution; how to acquire and refine skills for solving problems; how to transfer what is learned from situation to situation.

In social programmes, communication and education together lead to increased public participation in problem-solving and in activities which promote change. The participation of many individuals over time can lead to changed expectations for individual behaviour and institutional practices.

The process of communication and education together might be thought of as the "heating up" of a society around an issue through the "saturation" of all available channels of communication. In a "hot" society, all channels of communication and the processes of individual and social change reinforce a message. From the perspective of designing an education and communication programme, this might be called the "saturation" approach to social change.

Example of 'Saturation'

A decade ago, research information about the link between smoking and chronic disease, particularly cancer and heart attack, was communicated to health professionals in a hostile environment where smoking was considered socially "in". But information campaigns by governments and cancer/heart associations put smoking on the public agenda. The result? Conversations about smoking increased within households, doctors' offices and in laboratories. Community organisations began to take action. Schools and the work place joined in.

No-smoking campaigns became a catalyst for change in attitudes and behaviour in health with "smoking" as a unifying symbol. Under the umbrella of "smoking", the rituals and behaviours associated with smoking were individually affected by the saturation process. Therefore other health activities related to smoking also reaped the benefits. Extending the impact of saturation can be applied to other contexts.

Today, a new global image is emerging—an image which represents the environment and unifies people behind its common cause. The symbol of a "Green" earth and the colour "green" are perpetuating an environmental movement, the result of and an inspiration to environmental education and communication efforts everywhere.

"Green" political parties are gaining popular support. All over the world "green" label marketing approaches are influencing consumer behaviour. Just as in the smoking example, acting upon the unifying symbol of "green" through environmental education and communication has the potential to strengthen programmes and further heat up public consciousness. Environmental education and communication provides the opportunity to support policy change, institutional change and behaviour change in highly segmented audiences.

Stage 1: Setting the Public Agenda

Globally, the public is already talking about the environment. Numerous single-issue environmental groups and educational programmes are already in operation. People become ready to talk about, think about and support environmental activities. Membership in existing environmental groups increases, and new programmes and opportunities for popular participation appear.

Stage 2: Engaging Key Institutions

Building alliances and collaboration among institutions creates a network. Lead institutions reach out to other institutions representing social process—education, work, religion and government—and initiate collaborative educational activities. For example, school systems integrate environmental modules within existing curricula and initiate teacher training and youth ecoclubs. Community based action increasingly addresses local issues such as garbage collection and industrial pollutants. Media coverage responds more frequently and positively.

Stage 3: Establishing a New Environmental Order

Governmental and non-governmental institutions become the initiators of environmental education, and participation becomes broader and more diverse. Specific target audiences begin to modify their role with regard to particular environmental problems. Community mobilisation increasingly generates demand for appropriate regulatory change. Expectations for appropriate individual and social behaviour begin to change. Finally, "Green" positions become "in", "non-Green" positions "out".

Applied Research

Experience with development communication in other sectors leads to optimism in reaching new levels of excellence in combining environmental education and communication. Perhaps the most important element in "putting it all together", however, is to maintain commitment to well-tried applied research procedures.

- Investigation of target audience characteristics (including socio-economic, gender and cultural) and attributes (attitudinal and behavioural) in relation to local environmental issues provides insight into an appropriate model of behaviour change and effective educational strategies, messages and materials.
- Limited testing of innovative strategies devised for local situations will uncover refinements needed for broader application.
- Comparison studies between the impact of different educational strategies with similar objectives will provide a basis for future strategic choices.
- Standardised indicators of impact and evaluation studies will provide an assessment of the progress and impact of programmes and, to some extent, the relative power of different components within the programmes.
- Content analyses of mass media over time will provide profiles of societies "heating up" on environmental issues.
- Description of the differences between industrialised country and developing country objectives, programme content and impact will provide a source of new insight about the process of social and individual change.

In addition, applied research can also advance the state of the art for environmental education and communication when properly field tested. There are two major sources for such innovation:

1. the refinement of social change theory at universities and research firms;
2. "creative" concepts with proved efficacy in other sectors such as the "enter-educate" approach (education through entertainment) in the population sector.

This description of the potential and progress of environmental education and communication is, in reality, a call to action. The "heating up" of societies on environmental issues is technically within our reach through environmental education and communication programmes. It is up to us to develop the funding, the research-based strategies—and the communication among professionals about results, both successes and failure—required to make it happen.

Chapter 22

Beyond Economics

Unless policy-makers take a more all-round view of education, they risk sending their countries down the wrong path. Over the past decade, educational change in most countries has been driven by one imperative: survival in the global economy. This process has been particularly salient in the Asia-Pacific region following the drastic shock of the 1997 economic downturn. But in the current reform process, marked by speeding commercialisation and economic preoccupations, other educational missions are being ignored, and countries risk paying a high price for their short-sightedness.

There's no denying that economic considerations are critical in today's world. Students have to acquire the knowledge and skills to survive and compete in the global economy, especially one which more than ever before prizes human capital. A high-quality labour force gives nations a cutting edge in global competition. Understandably, stressing economic returns in the current educational debate attracts private resources. But education has other functions that are the indispensable corollary of more balanced, equitable development. They deserve to be briefly explained.

The first is a social function: education has a role to play in facilitating social mobility and bringing about integration in often very diverse constituencies. It is at school that children learn how to form a broader set of relationships, to live together and become aware of belonging to teach us civic attitudes, to make us aware of our rights and responsibilities—in essence, to become responsible citizens. The task is fundamental in light of democracy's advance in so many countries over the past decade or so. Then there is education's cultural function. Developing creativity and aesthetic awareness, accepting other traditions and belief systems while valuing our own are all part of the path towards fulfilment. Finally, education is a goal in and of itself. Schools help children learn how to learn and play a pivotal role in transferring knowledge from one generation to the next. I believe that all these facets of learning are critical for the long-term prosperity of our societies. In our globalised, interdependent world, these functions take on a more international character. Everywhere, education has a role to play in eliminating racial and gender biases, promoting global common interests, moments for peace, and greater international understanding.

Rising Above Short-Term Pressures to Strike a Harmonious Balance

While education is widely recognised as the spine of the learning society, the complexity lies in striking a balance between these various functions. The commercialisation of education that we are witnessing the world over inevitably pushes schools, educators, parents and policy-makers to pursue short-term, market-driven outcomes. Lawyers, bankers and businessmen have an increasingly high profile in educational debates. Following Southeast Asia's downturn in 1997, they were influential in changing the academic mindset. In little time, emphasis has shifted from academic achievement to developing communication skills, creativity, adaptability. In and of itself this is not necessarily regrettable. The problem is that these skills are all perceived to be at the service of a supreme economic value.

Sounder research will be required to analyse and assess where the current trends are leading us. It is increasingly recognised, however, that unless economic growth is accompanied by good governance, a fair sharing of benefits, better social and environmental protection and attention to culture, it will, sooner or later, lead to unrest. It is through education that this broad spectrum of concerns can be nurtured. Policy-makers who have taken stock of this holistic mission unfortunately represent a minority in today's educational debates and reforms. Their foremost challenge is to manage commercialisation, to rise above short-term pressures and to take a more ethical stance towards education, a long-term strategic view.

Chapter 23

Population Growth and Jobs

Since mid-century, the world's labour force has more than doubled, from 1.2 billion people to 2.7 billion, outstripping the growth in job creation. As a result, the United Nations International Labour Organisation estimates that nearly 1 billion people, approximately 30 per cent of the global work force, are unemployed or underemployed (working but not earning enough to meet basic needs). Over the next half-century, the world will need to create more than 1.9 billion jobs—all of them in the developing world—just to maintain current levels of employment.

As economists often note, while population growth may boost labour demand (through economic activity and demand for goods), it will most definitely boost labour supply. During the next 50 years, almost 40 million people will enter the global labour force—defined as those between the ages of 15 and 65 seeking work—each year. Between 1995 and 2050, some 1.9 billion additional jobs will need to be created to absorb these new would be workers. The most pressing needs will be found in the world's poorest nations—a sobering example of the vicious cycle linking poverty and population growth.

As the children of today represent the workers of tomorrow, the interaction between population growth and jobs is most acute in nations with young populations. Nations such as Peru, Mexico, Indonesia, and Zambia with more than half their population below the age of 25 will feel the burden of this labour flood. In the Middle East and Africa, 40 per cent of the population is under the age of 15. Since new entrants into the labour force were born at least 15 years ago, measures to reduce population growth have a delayed effect on the growth of the labour force, highlighting the urgency of taking action on population.

Nowhere is the employment challenge greater than in Africa, where at least 40 per cent of the population lives in absolute poverty. Although 8 million people entered the Sub-Saharan workforce in 1997, by 2030 this resource-scarce region will have to absorb more than 17 million new entrants each year. Over the next half-century, Nigeria's labour force is projected to grow by 246 per cent and Ethiopia's will soar by 337 per cent—both faster than growth of the general population. At current growth rates, the size of the labour force in Sub-Saharan Africa will more than triple by 2050.

As a result of unprecedented population growth and increasing acceptance of female participation in the workforce, the number of people seeking jobs in the Middle East and North Africa, a region already plagued by double-digit unemployment rates, will double in the next 50 years. In Algeria, where unemployment stands at 22 per cent, the labour force is growing at a staggering 4.2 per cent annually, and the number seeking work will more than double by 2050. Egypt alone will need to create 26 million more jobs by 2050 as its total population hits 115 million.

Nations throughout Asia will also see phenomenal increases in the numbers seeking work, including Pakistan, where the workforce will grow from 70 million in 1998 to 205 million by 2050. Over the next 25 years, India will add nearly 10 million to its work force each year. During the same period, China will add nearly 6 million annually due to population growth alone, compounding the work shortages caused by the current flood of migrants to China's coastal cities and by massive layoffs—estimated at more than 30 million—as state-run operations are scaled back.

Nations are hard-pressed to educate and train rapidly growing numbers of young people in marketable skills for the global workplace. Moreover, meeting the basic needs of a growing population draws scarce foreign exchange and other resources from investments in education and job creation. Throughout the world, young people entering the work force are increasingly faced with unemployment and social marginalisation. In most societies, unemployment rates for those under 25 are substantially higher than for older people.

Surplus farmland once served as a traditional source of employment for growing populations, as new land could be ploughed to generate work and income. However, global per capita Greenland has dropped by half and considerably more in certain nations since 1950. Moreover, the mechanisation of agriculture fuels the exodus of job seekers into the world's urban areas, where unemployment is often most acute, heavily reliant on natural capital in the past, future job creation will require massive amounts of financial capital to jump-start the industrial and service sectors.

As the balance between the demand and supply of labour is tipped by population growth, wages—the price of labour—tend to decrease. And in a situation of labour surplus, the quality of jobs may not improve as fast for workers will settle for longer hours, fewer benefits and less control over work activities.

Employment is the key to obtaining food, housing, health services, and education, in addition to providing self-respect and self-fulfilment. Rising numbers of unemployed people could drive global poverty and hunger to precarious levels, fueling political instability.

Chapter 24

Violence in School

A Worldwide Affair

In all countries, schools are magnets for strife in society, dealing with these tensions calls for extreme caution, for fear of making matters worse. Violence in schools is a world wide problem: it exists in rich and poor countries alike. It's chiefly a male phenomenon, hitting a peak when boys turn 16 years old in some countries and 13 in others. Experts agree at least on one point: this violence cannot be pinned to a single cause. Instead, they point to complex patterns linked to family situations. Socio-economic conditions and teaching methods.

Tackling Segregation

But these are just indicators and do not justify any deterministic explanations. When researchers say that 10 to 20 per cent of risk factors are linked to single parent families, this suggests that 80 to 90 per cent of such families are not the source of any violence. A child from a slum area with a teenage mother or a father in jail will not automatically be violent! Likewise, experts say there is a "hard core" of violent children—about five per cent of the total. One can found that this figure can vary between one and 11 per cent. The school itself can be an aggravating factor, though high staff turnover or "ghetto classes" to which poorly-performing students are relegated. These "hard core" groups, then cannot be deemed "inalterable". On the contrary, something can be done about them.

Should they simply be expelled, as some advocate? Such a measure would only make their segregation and sense of exclusion worse. And they are, after all, at the root of the whole problem. The solution lies partly in developing customized projects, but most importantly, in strengthening economic social participation.

To put an end to school violence, we need a well-established state with the means to compensate for inequalities, a state that tries to re-establish diversity in neighbourhoods and schools, one that does not give up on the notion of justice for children, as some are demanding.

Passing the Torch

We should also try to life schools out of their fortresses, so they do not become the symbol of a society that excludes people. Projects in the Netherlands, Brazil and the and the United States have shown that schools can be vibrant places that provide social, medical and cultural services to a neighbourhood.

In the Brazilian state of Minas Gerais, for example, there is a vocational school where elderly craftsmen teach their skills to teenagers. Such contact between generations can offer a very valuable social education. "It takes a village to educate a child", goes an effort an African proverb. Let's make an effort to seek out these opportunities, even in the most heartless cities.

Chapter 25

Helping Your Child Learn

A one-syllable word begins the education process: "Why?" Parents are always trying to answer that question. And that interaction between parent and child is the basis of much that children learn.

Teaching and learning are not mysteries that can happen only in school. They can also happen when parents and children do simple things together—things such as:

- Figure out whose socks are whose—sorting is a major function in maths and science.
- Cook a meal to learn science and good health.
- Tell each other a story as an important beginning for reading and writing; if the story is about the past, it's a way to interest a child in history.
- Plan a visit to a friend or relative for a personal connection with geography.
- Or play a game of hopscotch to develop counting and lifelong fitness.
- All children love their friends. So ask your child to describe his friend's appearance at the end of each school day. You can ask questions like. "What outfit did he/she wear?" or "How did he/she do his/her hair?" This

kind of routine query would encourage your child to observe his friend more minutely.

- If your child goes to school by bus, he can be asked to describe his route and point out certain landmarks namely colourful posters, traffic signals, large shops etc.

By doing things with their children, parents show that learning is fun and important—and that encourages children to study, learn, and stay in school.

Even on the discipline front, parents can help their children. Basic disciplinary principles must be tailored to each child and family. Before parents can become effective disciplinarians, they must first learn how to manage their own anger, solve problem situations and give and get support from others. Simple self-help techniques with or without professional support can help parents sharply reduce discipline problems.

Parents who are sensitive to their children's needs have more obedient children. Praise and love alone are not enough to instil good behaviour. Too much permissiveness hurts a child's efforts to develop self-control.

Behaviour problems should be reversed early. Waiting until the preteenage years diminishes chances for success and puts children at higher risk for drug use and other problems.

Parents need to learn as many tricks of the trade as possible, including how to play with their children, communicate with them, praise and reward them and also set limits for them, as well as how to handle misbehaviour using a variety of techniques.

All that parents need to help their children is a willingness to observe and learn with them, and, to take the time to nurture their natural curiosity.

Chapter 26

What's Driving Migration

The scale and diversity of today's migrations are beyond any previous experience. Rapid urban growth and environmental degradation in rural areas have led to internal migration affecting hundreds of millions of people. Migration is now seen as a priority issue equal in political weight to other major global challenges such as the environment, population growth and economic imbalances between regions.

Families and households form the basis for economic growth, social development and personal fulfillment. Decisions, by individual women and men on marriage, family, a place to live, shape the destinies of communities and nations. National policies and international conditions provide the context for individual decision-making. Effective development policies, including population, reproductive health and family planning policies, address this reality.

Data on national and global population trends set the agenda for national policy. An important element of population programmes is gathering data that will allow policy-making responsive to the realities of daily life, and to the needs and aspirations of individuals.

The dominant feature of global demographics is still growth. Age distribution is a growing concern, as the numbers of young and elderly people, grow, relative to the working-age population. The world is growing steadily more urban. From being a sign of strength and dynamism in the national economy, the rate and scale of urban growth has become increasingly a cause for concern. The influx of migrants to the biggest cities may be weakening both urban and rural sectors.

International migration is small in extent compared with internal movements, but has a disproportionate impact. Both internal and international migration are driven by population growth, and by inequities between countries. Migration is one of the choices which shape people's lives and the destiny of nations. But it can also be a symptom of inequity and underdevelopment. Migrants are by definition the most vulnerable members of the host community. Their living and working conditions should be protected.

Open and frank exchange of information and views between host and sending countries is needed more than ever. The aim of the international community should be to protect the right to move, but to ensure that movement is voluntary and that it stimulates rather than holds back personal and national development. "The point of departure should be the human right to live and work where one pleases, so long as it does not infringe on other people's rights to do the same."

The Urban Transformation

The rural sector is declining in importance and its contribution to national economies. It is increasingly part of a unified economy based on the city. Contact with the urban areas is easier than ever and is encouraged by rural development.

Temporary and circular migration is giving way to more permanent settlement. The largest cities are under increasing strain, and residents are encountering increasing difficulties in improving or even maintaining living conditions. Nevertheless, migration continues, driven by a variety of forces both positive and negative. The choice to move can be part of a strategy for survival or personal development; but it is often enforced by external conditions.

The urban transformation is irreversible, but the rural sectors must also be strengthened to balance the developing economy. Attention to gender issues will be crucial in ensuring a successful transition. The forces driving internal and international migration have much in common. Demographic pressures are contributing to both. As the pressures encouraging migration increase, the options for migrants become more limited. This collision is contributing to the atmosphere of crisis surrounding both urban and international migration.

Costs and Benefits

Migration is the result of individual or family decisions. But it is also part of social process. In economic terms, migration is as much a global phenomenon as trade in commodities or manufactured goods. It is part of a broader pattern, and evidence of changing economic, social and cultural relationships.

But migration may be evidence of a different kind of relationship; the combination of poverty, rapid population growth and environmental damage is a powerful destabilizing factor driving urban growth and eventually international migration. On the recipient side, migration has usually been seen as evidence of a thriving economy; today's industrial states were built in part by migrant labour, skills and investment. In today's increasingly uncertain conditions, migration may be seen as a threat to the security and well-being of the local workforce and society at large.

The only effective means to reduce migration pressures over the long term are to slow population growth; to stimulate economic growth and job creation at home, and promote the development of the individual and the family as the basic economic and social unit.

A Question of Gender

It is often assumed that most migrants are men, in reality, women make up nearly half of the international migrant population. Gender differences in social and economic roles affect migration decision-making, household strategy, and the sex composition of labour migration. Attention to the gender dimension of migratory movements ought to be an important component in population and development planning.

Women frequently take the initiative in migration decisions, which may reflect limited opportunities in rural areas. Low status limits women's choices at home and may increase pressure to migrate, but it may also affect life in the host community. Opportunities may be limited by lack of education or skills, or by customer limitation on women's freedom of action outside the family or ethnic group. Paid employment for migrant women is usually in the lowest wage, least secure, and lowest status jobs, mostly in housework, child care and trade.

Most educated women end up in the same low-status, low-wage production and service-jobs as unskilled female migrants. Men too, experience downward mobility, but the contrast in the decline in women's employment status is far greater. Despite these disadvantages women migrants have become significant economic actors. Their status may be improved by migration, but the advantages are not clear-cut. Women's status as migrants is affected by their vulnerability, and by their lack of reproductive freedom. To ensure improved status they will need both legal protection and essential services, including reproductive health services.

Refugees

Refugees in the 1990s are overwhelmingly in Asia, Africa and Latin America. Their numbers are large, about 17 million, and growing rapidly. A further 3.5 to 4 million were thought to be in "refugee-like situation", though estimates are probably extremely conservative, and an estimated 23 million people internally displaced.

It is important to recognize the common roots of refugees and other forms of mass movement of populations. At the same time, despite the difficulty of distinguishing between political and socio-economic causes of migration, there is a clear need to distinguish between refugees and other groups of migrants. Participation in international efforts of burden-sharing would ensure that most refugee problems would be dealt within their regions of origin.

Conclusions and Policies

Migration highlights linkages and interdependencies within countries, with many implications for development agendas, including population programmes and development assistance.

Policies to regulate or moderate international migration have concentrated largely on urban growth. They have been only intermittently effective. The most successful have concentrated on stimulating rural development and the growth of alternative urban centres.

Migration is also a personal or family decision, which is affected by external conditions such as poverty or environmental degradation, improving conditions of personal and family life can make a crucial difference in the decision to migrate, reducing dependence on migration as a strategy. Because migration is the result of personal and family decisions, it can be influenced by policies that improve the quality of life.

This offers the opportunity for policies emphasizing individual development, among them education, health (including reproductive health) and family planning. Such policies are particularly relevant to the strategies must take into account gender differences in social and economic life and the differential effects of policies.

Migration decisions are about family security and long-term-life-chances, rather than simply the maximisation of income. They are ultimately strategies designed to look after the individual's and the household's needs, safeguard their security, and respond to their aspirations. If the goal is to reduce migration pressures through development it will be essential to increase the capacity but reduce the need to migrate. Long-term external support will be required to make such policies a reality, particularly in areas of rapid population growth and potential mass outward flows. Highly co-ordinated allocation of development assistance can be help establish priorities and focus attention on basic needs. The challenge to both international donors and co-operating governments is to direct programme spending to the areas where it can be most effective.

Chapter 27

Technological Entrepreneurship

The New Force for Economic Growth

Entrepreneurship has emerged as a major new force for change. The dynamic role of modern small business in economic growth has received fresh recognition worldwide. It is essential to promote entrepreneurship and to mobilize the dynamism of the private sector for accelerated national development. An unbridled private sector may not, however, ensure growth with equity. It is the prime responsibility of governments to create policy frameworks that enable business to apply technology for competitive advantage and for the well-being of the public.

The Changing Global Environment

As agents of change and progress, entrepreneurs start by identifying a market opportunity and matching this with social or technical innovations. They then proceed to mobilize the resources necessary to drive their business concept to its commercial realisation. The development of a product or service with a high-technology content—never easy anywhere, or at today's rapidly-changing global environment. It calls for restructuring the available technology and business development systems and developing the skills needed by a new breed of "techno-entrepreneurs" to transform innovations into market opportunities at home and abroad. It also requires reorienting the present processes and priorities of technical and economic cooperation among countries.

Amidst the global concerns of environmental preservation, poverty elimination and social development, the practical problems of entrepreneurship are not being properly addressed, even though entrepreneurs will create the bulk of enterprises, jobs and wealth.

A torrent of technology-based goods hits the market every week, ostensibly improving the quality of our lives while simultaneously creating complexity and dislocation. The pace of progress in information technologies, microelectronics, robotics, new materials, biomedical sciences, space science and other advanced technologies quickens, significantly changing the way we live. The growth of markets for these technologies also proceeds apace.

Further, technological change is taking place today against a background of growing intra-national and international disequilibria. While the transformation from State-centred to market-oriented development is opening up enormous opportunities and options, it has also caused severe short-term hardships. In order to survive and prosper in these changing times, India and its enterprises need enlightened government policies, good technical infrastructure and strong cultural roots.

Traditional production factors are giving way to a new paradigm characterised by new patterns of trade, investment and employment, and by informal networking life-long learning and technological entrepreneurship. The manufacturing sector in India continues to be dominated by food products, textiles, chemicals and other traditional industry, mainly in the public sector. However, change is coming, albeit slowly. State enterprises are being corporatised pending privatisation, and the share of knowledge-based and information-related activities in the marketplace is rising perceptibly. Restructuring policies now place emphasis (often purely rhetorical) on the role of the private sector. The legacy of decades of centrally-planned development is generally inimical to private enterprise. In turn, the private sector has been slow to respond to economic liberalisation in India and generally failed to generate the new employment necessary to absorb new entrants to the labour force.

The regulatory problems of an onerous tax structure and administration, poor access to finance and raw materials, over-regulation of labour and land use, pervasive bureaucracy and restricted markets have been significant barriers to entrepreneurial growth.

Towards Competitive Performance

The imperative of improved performance has serious implications for India if it is to survive, stay abreast and succeed. It calls for national efforts on systemic efficiency and productivity growth, the move from an investment-driven to an innovation-driven economy and sustained higher-order competitiveness; towards enhanced customer satisfaction at home and penetration of selected markets abroad. Concurrently, governments and business have to address such intractable problems as poverty, corruption and the degradation of the environment.

Creating New Technology-Based Ventures

Starting a new business in India is a hazardous task. Problems are compounded when the venture is technology-based:

- Capital requirements are generally larger, while traditional banks are ill-equipped to process the perceived risk. Venture capital generally only becomes an option when the venture has documented the merits of its management, market and innovation.
- Knowledge-based ventures can benefit from linkages to sources of knowledge—e.g. the technical university or research lab. Such mentoring needs to be cultivated.

- Techno-entrepreneurs often have technical skills but usually lack the business management and marketing skills necessary for success. These need to be supplemented.
- In fields where technology is changing rapidly, it is often advantageous to make technology-acquisition arrangements. Sourcing such innovations, negotiating technology licensing agreements and protecting the intellectual property itself require special skills.
- Knowledge-based innovations are inherently more risky than others. The management of this unique risk requires assessment techniques and vision.
- Technology-based ventures often have social and environmental implications, which need to be managed carefully.
- Penetrating a competitive market requires good market intelligence, a good strategic plan and good luck.

Special Characteristics of "Techno-entrepreneurs"

The popular misconceptions are that techno-entrepreneurs are born, not made; that they take risks with other people's money and fail more often than they succeed. In fact, entrepreneur skills can be identified and developed. The entrepreneur is typically an innovator who formulates new solutions to existing problems, mobilizes resources and stimulates others to participate in his or her team. These aptitudes develop over time, often starting in childhood, as the person faces new challenges and learns from failure.

Entrepreneurial opportunities can be found in every industrializing country, community and family. Principal sources of entrepreneurs for knowledge-based ventures are often the university and government research laboratories, the large industrial and military establishments and professional service firms. Some motivations of the entrepreneur are the need to: be independent; create value; contribute to society; earn recognition; become rich or; quite often, simply not to be unemployed. Value-adding ventures with good growth potential can best be developed in an open market and in a culture which supports risk-taking.

The techno-entrepreneur anywhere has the challenge of moving a concept through the prototype and production phases towards creation of a product which meets market needs at a price consistent with the value created and with the ability of customers to pay.

Equally important, the market itself has to be developed and sustained. It is not enough to be first with a better mousetrap if one does not have the skills to educate and reach potential buyers and to set the market standard.

Hence one has to distinguish between innovators and inventors. The inventor is typically a creative person in a quest for knowledge or for producing new products, without determining in advance whether a real market exists for his or her inventions. On the other hand, the innovator draws on existing knowledge and the talents of others to develop or adapt a product or service at a volume and cost that can capture a significant portion of an identified market. The flexibility and creativity of a small entrepreneurial techno-venture may lead to more incremental and break through innovations than can be generated by larger-sized firms in many sectors.

The pace and pattern of India's economic development now depend in large measure on its technical resource base. In this context, the key determinants are the skills to apply technology for enhanced competitiveness, as well as to create techbased ventures. Techno-entrepreneurs have to be supported by appropriate national structures and international linkages if they are to survive and flourish in an intensely competitive world.

Chapter 28

In Defence of the City Urban Development a Key for Survival

The figures sound alarming. The towns and cities in developing countries are growing faster than ever before. By the year 2000, 2.2 billion people will live in the cities of the Third World. Their numbers are expected to double by the year 2025. But many of the cities in Africa, Asia and Latin America are already bursting at the seams. Some of the so-called megacities have more than 10 or 15 million inhabitants. Many of them live in unplanned squatter settlements, without water and electricity, in an environment of squalor, poverty, crime and disease. Nevertheless, the cities seem to have lost nothing of their attraction for the rural populations. Although the larger share of the population increase in the cities of developing countries is caused by the children of people already living there, the rural-urban migration continues unabated. The cities still offer better chances for employment and education, they provide a better physical infrastructure, better health facilities and a more interesting life. Miserable as conditions in the cities often appear to be, they are usually much better than those in the rural areas. It is, therefore, an illusion to believe that the growth of the cities could be checked by concentrating the development efforts on the countryside. There is no alternative to urban development in a world will soon count some 8 billion people.

Cities have always been in the vanguard of development. The ancient civilisations of Mesopotamia, Egypt, Greece and Rome were city cultures which for the first time in human development created large, well-governed states. In Europe during the Middle Ages, the creation of towns and cities offered the rural populations a chance to evade the oppression by feudal authorities and become free citizens. Local self-government in medieval towns is at the cradle of democratic development. There is a clear separation of competence between the national, state and local level of government leaving citizens an opportunity to decide on matters which directly affect their own local environment. It is worth looking at this model when discussing ways organised to improve city governance and allow for more participation of the population.

Another fact worth looking at is the size of cities in Industrialised countries. Although about three quarters of the people live in urban areas, there are only a handful of really big cities.

Of course, the growth of towns and cities in developed countries is the result of a long historical process, deeply rooted in the particular political and economic conditions of the past centuries. In developing countries today, other conditions prevail which favour the emergence of ever bigger urban conglomerations. However, governments are able, thorough appropriate investments and the location of industries educational facilities or housing policies to influence the settlement trends in their respective countries in favour of smaller cities.

One point seems certain, though, when considering the pros and cons of city development: the severe environmental problems facing mankind today can only be solved if people live in highly concentrated settlements rather than being spread out evenly over the whole countryside. Environment-friendly mass transport, for instance, is only possible in the cities. Fossil fuel consumption which adds to the pollution of the atmosphere will be lower when people live close to their places of work. Their supply with food, water, electricity and social amenities is cheaper and uses up fewer resources when distances are short. The use of land for housing, transport and industry is less when buildings grow in height rather than space. Even refuse disposal and wastewater management is easier to organise in a big city than in the countryside.

What is important then is not to question the validity of city development, but to make cities and tows a better place to live in. Good city governance, more involvement of the population in decision-making, more attention paid to environmental hazards caused by congestion and low safety standards are some of the demands that must be met to cope with the problems of the cities. There is no reason to bedevil the city as the most successful form of human settlement. Since the times of Babylon, it has also been a place where many different peoples and cultures meet. A generation from now, half the human population will live in cities. We should see this as a chance for human survival.

Chapter 29

Aid Effectiveness as a Multi-level Process

Parallel to the widespread decrease of aid resources provided by donor countries to developing countries in recent years, debate and research on how to make aid more effective has become a major concern. Usually, it is suggested that decades of development assistance have at best produced marginal results in terms of improving development levels in the South. Little mention is made of donor's policy shortcomings and the negative impact of these on efforts aimed at reforming and redefining development cooperation in order to enhance aid effectiveness. The policy parameters and operating frameworks of existing aid policies continue to inhibit higher degrees of aid effectiveness. In many donor countries, opinion polls indicate waning public support for development aid.

Increasingly, the moral case for aid is called into question and deeper world market integration tends to be seen as the panacea to continued economic decline and social destabilisation in the South. Against this background, cooperation between donor and recipient actors is faced with a duel uphill struggle. First, fewer resources can be mobilised to meet growing developmental needs. On the other hand, to organise and manage development policies and programmes in a result-oriented manner, grows more difficult. The threat of further aid cuts and of further drops of public support for providing aid become ever more real. A closer look at the organisational complexities and political constraints under which development cooperation is expected to perform effectively may help to improve current aid management approaches.

Towards Conceptual Clarity

At first sight, catchy definitions of what constitutes effective aid might appear attractive to use, in particular with regard to economic indicators. The term "aid effectiveness" is easily used in the same vein as "efficiency", "significance" or "impact" of aid. At times, obsession to measure and demonstrate the results of aid supported development processes can be observed among policy-makers and administrators on the donor side. Still the understanding of aid and its effectiveness as being part and parcel of a cooperation relationship between donor and recipient side parties, is scarcely embedded in practice. To determine how to make aid more effective requires more than a quick impact analysis of an individual and perhaps even isolated development project. Consequently, defining the concept of aid effectiveness needs to take into account at what levels cooperation is focused on. To strive for sustainable and effective modes of development cooperation will entail the need to combine recipient ownership of the development process with donor accountability concerns.

Performance expectations cannot be exclusively placed on the recipient while donor interests, their aid management systems and procedures remain unchanged.

An extended and more analytical, process-oriented definition should take into account four main aspects of aid effectiveness:

(a) Effective aid must relate to the building and/or strengthening of in-country aid management capacity;

(b) To maximise the degree of aid effectiveness, local ownership of the aid process is essential: from setting

of priorities through policy formulation and implementation on to the evaluation stages of the process;

(c) Increasing recipient side capabilities to take charge of aid relationship, will need to be combined with arrangements to meet legitimate donor accountability concerns;

(d) Aid effectiveness is a two-faceted objective: its realisation is equally dependent on increased transparency of donor motives and on dropping of non-developmental, political and economic aid objectiveness of donors.

In addition a broader range of stakeholders in the aid relationship needs to be actively involved: extending beyond accountable government and implementing agencies, to include democratic institutions and organisations of civil society and of the private sector.

Applying any definition of aid effectiveness without disaggregating macro-economic data and taking into account country specificity will only lead to unhelpful generalisations about aid and its effectiveness. It would seem more appropriate to adopt working definitions against which to assess effectiveness of aid resources at a country-specific level. On such a basis one could expect to arrive at more reliable indicators of how well aid resources contribute to improving developmental standards and meeting existing needs.

From Definition to Success—Key Requirements

Having reached agreement between the recipient and donor on what should constitute effectiveness of aid is only a starting point. Embarking on democratic, peaceful and participatory patterns of economic and social development must follow: to arrive at significant and lasting improvement in many of the least developed countries will be a long-term process. This being said, it is crucial to design and implements such forms of development cooperation which involve a wide range of recipient side actors, not only from the government side but also from civil society at large. Seen as a process of increasing inclusion of intended beneficiaries of aid, the commitment to decentralise as well as entrust aid and its management grows in importance.

To fully capture Third World development realities, policy frameworks inspired by neoliberalist-type of development concepts and theories are grossly inadequate. The views and positions on aid articulated in the World Bank and the IMF, or in many if not most bilateral aid administrations in OECD countries, represent only one side of today's international cooperation, namely the donor side. The major weakness to point out with respect to this locus of debate, is a profound under representation if not even a total absence of recipient experiences and perceptions on aid in general and on its effectiveness in particular. There should be little doubt that ignoring to not actively identifying and involving such perceptions, leads to strongly donor driven aid.

To circumvent recipient side insights and views on strengths and weaknesses of aid strategies and mechanisms, will result in limited local commitment and sense of ownership over the aid process. Mutual decision-making between donors and recipients remains a rare policy approach. Aid procedures that are based on local management and less control-oriented donor roles in the aid process are still exceptions in development cooperation.

Structurally, in terms of the policy environment within which development aid is expected to function, the overriding policy framework is general based on structural adjustment policies (SAP). But the underlying conclusion made by proponents of SAPs that these policies induce aid effectiveness, has yet to be proven valid. It must suffice at this point to emphasize that there is no *a priori* relationship between world market integration under structural adjustment and sustainable development in poor countries.

Aid to these countries which is solely intended to reinforce fundamentally uneven and unequal patterns of world market integration should be scrutinised critically.

Some central issues need to be addressed in the course of improving aid and its effectiveness:

- institutional dimensions of aid relationships require strong policy-attention, both on the donor and the recipient side;
- capacities to effectively identify and formulate aid priorities need to be strengthened in recipient countries;
- local capacities to sustain reform efforts must be reinforced.

Levels of Intervention

If the design of aid and the terms upon which it is provided to a developing country are largely determined by the donor, the aid relationship can be characterised as essentially hierarchical. Recipient side views will rarely surface, as they are either not identified, or not well formulated. Possibilities of a recipient-led development strategies can be limited. Unless scope is provided to the recipient side actors to assume responsibilities, aid effectiveness is likely to remain low or fluctuating, and the sustainability of donor aid efforts will remain doubtful.

National planning processes and courses of national development in recipient countries should be seen as most effective where they are led under local responsibility and control. To arrive at this ideal situation, gaps need to be reduced and closed at the various intervention levels.

Donor aid resources provide valuable support for this process. Their effectiveness in meeting long-term objective of aid will need to be assessed on the basis of how well they perform at the different levels. Individual donors will expectedly perform differently at the various levels. What will prove to be the ultimate test for effectiveness is how well the donor aid performance accomplishes the broader objectives of development cooperation and how well it includes sustainable results.

In the analytical frameworks outlined here, development cooperation would seem to be confronted with the effectiveness gaps at the:

- *Structural Level:* International trade and investment patterns, debt problems and world market integration process appear as long-term constraining factors upon aid and its effectiveness;
- *Policy Level:* Dialogue and partnership in development cooperation are instrumental factors in recluding planning and co-ordination gaps with regard to policy analysis and formulation;
- *The Institutional Level* is where pertinent capacity gaps exist: capacity development efforts of donors and technical assistance measures play an important role in addressing weaknesses in aid effectiveness within a country's institutional setting;
- Finally, at the *level of aid projects* (programmes), it is generally the lack of sustainability of aid interventions which causes development activities to falter once donor support decreases or stops. In addition to technical cooperation, financial and material inputs serve to maintain project momentum and goal realisation. The issue of how to develop local capacity sufficiently in order for indigenous organisations to continue project activities initially supported by donor aid, remains the most important issue to address at this level.

Fostering Aid Effectiveness

Donor and recipient development efforts are too often isolated from one another, or poorly coordinated. They fail to address managerial and implementation bottlenecks. Cross-sectoral linkages, as well as interdisciplinary approaches to aid problems are only slowly gaining ground. It is increasingly obvious, that decisions on aid issues are subjected to concerns outside of the responsible ministry. Finance Ministers, and unfortunately even Defence Ministers have a strong say in how much aid is to be provided, where it is to be concentrated and under what terms to be utilised. Inside of recipient countries, large portions of national budgets are allocated to non-development priorities with little or no impact on alleviating urgent poverty problems.

Development cooperation may make the biggest impact and be executed most effectively where donors and recipients agree upon multi-level aid strategies. To give an example, building a road to a remote rural area may well be done in an effective project manner. It is equally important to have a functioning transport authority in place to ensure maintenance of the roads. If this authority operates within a nationally defined infrastructure policy, best in accord with national trade and investment priorities, then the effectiveness of the project-level road building programme has a good chance of being high.

Institutional changes to set the stage for a profound reform process in development cooperation are needed. Reprioritising national budgets to reflect identified in country development needs may be one step. Setting up policy evaluation and formulation units can be complimentary measures. Deregulating markets and investment rules may serve to please donors, but dumping of cheap products which strangle local production efforts may easily result. Regional cooperation, including intensified South-South cooperation can provide some counterbalance. There are only a few areas where changes in the current system of development cooperation can occur, with a view to better manage the complexities of aid and the social, cultural, economic and political backgrounds against which they take place. The will and commitment to take policy action in both donor and recipient countries, through the broadest range of stakeholders and institutions as possible, will be the test for genuine efforts at improving development relations between North and South and organising cooperation effectively.

Chapter 30

The WTO and the Developing Countries

The special status of developing countries in the GATT will continue to receive recognition in the WTO. The preamble of the Agreement establishing the WTO states that "there is a need for positive efforts designed to ensure that developing countries, and especially the least developed among them, secure a share in the growth of international trade commensurate with the needs of their economic development". In addition to retaining the provisions that concerned developing countries in GATT 1947, the new agreement generally contain provisions for developing countries and least-developed countries, often consisting of longer transition periods for the full implementation of some obligations and various exemptions from obligations, particularly for the latter group of countries. Also, in some instances, the exports of developing countries benefit from a better treatment with respect to measures taken by other WTO Members. Technical assistance is to be provided to developing countries to assist them in assuming their obligations and more effectively realising the benefits of the multilateral trading system.

Least-developed countries are singled out in the Final Act as requiring special attention. This is reflected in the Agreements through a number of provisions which provide the most favourable treatment for this group in terms of rights as well as lower levels of obligations. In addition, the Decision on Measures in Favour of Least-Developed Countries, makes provision for measures of special assistance, including technical assistance "in the development, strengthening and diversification of their production and export bases including those of services, as well as in trade promotion, to enable them to maximise the benefits from liberalised access to markets". As part of its functions, the Committee on Trade and Development (a subsidiary body of the General Council) will periodically review the special provisions in favour of least-developed countries and report to the General Council of the WTO for appropriate action.

The Declaration on the Contribution of the WTO to Achieving Greater Coherence in Global Economic Policy making identifies the need for strengthening the relationship between the activities of the WTO, the International Monetary Fund (IMF) and the World Bank as a way of ensuring greater coherence in global economic policy-making.

Market Access

Industrial Products: For developed countries, the main features of their market access commitments in industrial products include the expansion of bindings to cover 99 per cent of imports; the expansion of duty free access from 30 to 44 per cent of total imports; and the reduction of the trade-weighted average tariff by 40 per cent (i.e. from the per-Uruguay Round level of 6.2 per cent to the post-Uruguay Round level of 3.7 per cent). With respect to tariff reductions on individual product categories, developed countries will reduce tariffs by substantially above-average amounts (60 per cent or more) in three categories—wood, pulp, paper and furniture; metals; and non-electric machinery and reduce tariffs by less than the 40 per cent overall reduction in four categories—fish and fish products; textiles and clothing; leather, rubber, footwear; and transport equipment.

In terms of exports from developing to developed country markets, the total reduction in the average tariff of developed countries is 37 per cent. Below average tariff reductions, and above average levels of tariffs apply to labour-intensive manufacturers (textiles and clothing, leather goods) and certain processed primary products (fish products) that have been—and continue to be—regarded as "sensitive".

Developed countries constitute the most important merchandise exports markets for developing countries (62 per cent in 1992). In part, this is because the developed countries account for the bulk of global income and expenditures. At the same time, market access opportunities for developing countries in each other's markets have long been affected by the protection in their own markets. In many instances, the level of protection is quite high, because important protection, ultimately, acts as a tax on exports as well, protection in developing countries also hinders the integration of developing countries also hinders the integration of developing economies, not just with each other, but with the larger global trading system.

The reductions in bound tariffs which the new commitments of developing economies represent are difficult to assess for several reasons. The first is that comprehensive information on base (1986) tariffs is unavailable in many cases as a result of the low level of bindings among developing countries. In these cases, the post-Uruguay Round average bound tariff usually involves a decrease in the ceiling bindings applied to items already found, combined with ceiling bindings above currently applied rates for previously unbound items. Another reason is that, where developing economies had bound all or a significant portion of tariffs prior to the end of the Round, the Uruguay Round tariff commitments often reflect a decline in ceiling rates (rather than applied rates).

At the same time, current tariff levels already reflect the often substantial reductions undertaken autonomously in the course of the Round. Though many developing countries may not be required to introduce further cuts, previous liberalisation has been at least partly locked in through new commitments on bindings. Ceiling bindings are considered to be so important that countries which agree to bind previously unbound tariffs are given "negotiating credits" for the decision even if the tariff is bound at a level above the currently applied level (as is the case for many developing economy participants in the Round). Bindings have also played a key role in establishing the domestic and international credibility of domestic reform programmes in many countries. Although an integral part of the tariff negotiations, bindings clearly are more akin to rules and procedures—in terms of their contribution to the predictability of future market access—than to direct increases in market access. However, even ceiling bindings yield significant benefits related to liberalisation when they reduce the expect value and variance of protection.

On the basis of data available for 26 developing countries, the GATT Secretariat has identified the main features of their market access commitments. These include: the expansion of bindings to cover 61 per cent of imports, compared to the pre-Uruguay Round level of 13 per cent. The increase in the security of trade among developing regions is reflected mainly in Latin America—where participants will bind 100 per cent of tariff lines at ceilings rates.

Too often, "market access" as used in descriptions of the Uruguay Round results is defined—implicitly or explicitly in a way that is too narrow and, even worse, mercantilist. The narrowness results from limiting the analysis of changes in market access to changes in tariffs and quotas. This overlooks three other key aspects of market access, namely the bindings of tariffs, the rules and disciplines on the use of other trade-related government interventions, and the institutional arrangements for monitoring and enforcing compliance with those disciplines. It is progress in these latter three areas that determines the security of increases in market access from reductions in tariffs and the elimination of quantitative restrictions. Since the gains from trade liberalisation depend heavily on the stimulus it provides to trade-related investment, the security aspect is crucial.

Agricultural Products: Increased market access for agricultural products includes the "tariffication" of all non-tariff border measures (conversion to tariff-equivalents)—with the exception of those products for which special treatment has been negotiated—and a binding of all tariffs on agricultural products. As a result, the security of trade in agricultural products will for the first time be greater than in industrial products, since 100 per cent of agricultural product tariff lines will be bound.

Tariffs resulting from the "tariffication" process, together with the other tariffs on agricultural products, are to be reduced by a simple average of 36 per cent over six years in the case of developed countries and 24 per cent over ten years in the case of developing countries, with minimum reductions per tariff line of 15 per cent and 10 per cent, respectively. The reductions in the tariffs of developed countries—which account for about two-thirds of world imports of agricultural products—indicate an average percentage reduction of 37 per cent. With respect to individual product categories, developed countries will cut tariffs by above-average amounts on oilseeds, flowers an plants; and cut tariffs by below-average amounts on sugar and dairy products, with other product categories close to the average cut. In the categories of "topical products", which account for half of exports of developing countries of agricultural products, a 43 per cent reduction in tariffs will be implemented by developed countries.

Current access opportunities will be maintained on terms at least equivalent to those existing prior to the tariffication process. However, for those products where tariffication took place and imports were less than 5 per cent of domestic consumption because of the existing restrictions, minimum market access commitments, implemented through tariff quotas on an MFN basis at a low or minimal tariff rate, are required. Figures on the increased market access in terms of tonnage resulting from minimum access commitments indicate that substantial increases in market access occur for coarse grains (1,757,000 tons) and rice (1,076,000 tons), as well as for other products. With regard to commitments on export competition, the quantities of exports which can be legally subsidised must be reduced by 21 per cent. Furthermore, total export subsidy outlays will decline by 36 per cent, from $21.3 billion to $13.7 billion by the end of the transition period. The importance of this commitment is that, on average, developed countries subsidised annually during 1986-90 48.2 million tons of wheat, 19.5 million tons of coarse grains, 1.8 million tons of sugar, 1.2 million tons of beef, etc. With regard to commitments on domestic support to agricultural producers, total outlays (in terms of the Aggregate Measurement of Support) will be reduced by 18 per cent, from $197, billion to $162 billion by the end of the transition period.

The new market access opportunities for agricultural products which will result from the Uruguay Round—as a result of a change in border measures, and policies relating to export competition and domestic support—will be of particular interest to developing countries exporting temperature food products. More generally, multilateral discipliners on trade-distorting practices in agriculture are expected to stabilise world food markets in the coming decades, providing potential trade opportunities for developing countries and reducing fluctuations in food import bills. However, the potential situation in net food-importing developing countries is of particular concern. Potential problems relating to least-developed and net food importing developing countries are the subject of the Decision on *Measures Concerning the Possible Negative Effects of the Reform Programme on Least-Developed and Net Food Importing Developing Countries.* The decision sets out objectives with regard to the provision of food aid, the provision of basic foodstuffs in full grant form and aid for agricultural development. It also refers to the possibility of assistance from the International Monetary Fund and the World Bank with respect to the short-term financing of food imports. The WTO Committee of Agriculture will monitor the implementation of the decision.

WTO Agreements Covering Trade in Goods

GATT 1994: The cornerstone of trade relations in the area of goods. Differential and more favourable treatment to developing countries and to least-developed countries is permitted under the 1979 Enabling Clause with respect to tariffs in the context of the Generalised System of Preferences (GSP) and non-tariff measures, notwithstanding the most-favoured-nation clause, and with respect to regional or global arrangements concluded by developing countries.

Agreements Integrating Practices Otherwise on the Margin of GATT Rules: Includes Trade-Related Investment Measures (TRIMs) (which can be found to be inconsistent with the national treatment provision or the prohibition on quantitative restrictions), such as local content requirements or trade-balancing requirements. GATT inconsistent TRIMs are required to be notified and eliminated within a transition period of and two years (developed countries), five years (developing countries) or seven years (least-developed countries). A further extension may be requested by developing and least-developed countries. The Agreement on Safeguards prohibits the use of "grey-area measures", such as voluntary restraints or orderly marketing arrangements; such measures are to be notified and eliminated.

Agreement on Textiles and Clothing: Provides for the eventual elimination of the Multi-Fibre Arrangement (MFA) after a ten-year transition period. In place since 1973, the MFA currently groups eight "importers"; of these,

Austria, Canada, the European Communities, Finland, Norway and the United States apply restrictions under the MFA, while Japan and Switzerland do not. The other participants in the MFA are the "exporters" (mainly developing countries), whose exports or part of their exports covered by the MFA are subject to bilaterally agreed quantitative restraints or unilaterally imposed restraints on imports, typically applied at the product level but in some cases to various aggregates as wells.

Trade in Services

The General Agreement on Trade in Services (GATS) is the first multilateral agreement on trade that has its objective the progressive liberalisation of trade in services. It provide for secure and more open market in services in a similar manner as the GATT has done for trade in goods. The agreement covers trade in all service sectors and the supply of service in all forms.

The GATS has two components: the framework agreement containing 29 Articles and a number of Annexes, Ministerial Decisions etc., as well as the schedules of commitments undertaken by each member to bind the existing degree of openness or remove existing restrictions.

Of importance to developing countries is the fact that virtually all member have made commitments on the movement of natural persons, even if these are circumscribed by the requirement of intra-corporate transferee status. In addition, commitments made by developed countries generally cover the cross-border supply of labour-intensive services such as computer-related services, professional and construction services. Further, most developing countries have committed themselves to bind or liberalise tourism and travel service, including, for example, the liberalisation of foreign investment restrictions for hotel and resort operators. These commitments are likely to improve the supply capacity of this key sector, which provides the major source of foreign exchange earnings in a number of island developing countries and least-developed countries. In addition, a number of developing countries have taken the opportunity the GATS provides to schedule commitments, thereby binding their own domestic reform process. Improvements in the quality of service that will result from liberalisation and increased competition will contribute to improved efficiency, consumer welfare and growth in developing countries as well as all other countries.

Intellectual Property Rights

Under the WTO, the number of countries providing intellectual property protection will increase over time. Developed countries have one year to meet their obligations, developing countries have five years and least developed countries have eleven years, with the possibility of an extension. Special transitional arrangements apply in the situation where a developing country does not presently provide patent protection in a particular chemical.

Adherence to the Paris and Berne Conventions is fairly widespread among developing countries. Many developing countries already provide minimum standards of intellectual property protection on a national treatment basis, although the scope of such protection varies significantly. Potential benefits for developing countries emerging from the Uruguay Round include a framework more conducive to domestic research efforts and to technology transfer and foreign direct investment. There will, however, be additional administrative burdens on enforcing such rights (specifically dealt with under the TRIPs Agreement), potentially higher royalty payments and adjustment costs for industries which, in the absence of domestic legislation in the area, were producing goods that would be considered as counterfeit in the future. These will also be requirements relating to patents which may well mean an increase in prices of certain goods in some developing countries. Pharmaceutical and agricultural products present examples. These increases are expected to be small, and there are provisions in the Agreement itself to minimise any adverse implications for developing countries.

Dispute Settlement

From the perspective of developing countries, it should be noted that the elements of the 1966 Decision on Dispute Settlement will continue to apply under the WTO dispute settlement procedures. Although this Decision has seldom been used, mainly because developing countries have only recently become more frequent users of the GATT dispute settlement procedures, it contains features of specific interest to developing countries, including automatic access to the "good offices" of the Director-General of the GATT/WTO to mediate and seek to find a satisfactory resolution to the dispute, and shorter time-limits in which panels must complete their deliberations.

Monitoring of Trade Policies

The TPRM provide for a Trade Policies Review Body to examine regularly the trade policies and practices of Members, every two years for the four major traders (the EU, US, Japan and Canada), every four years for the next sixteen leading traders, and every six years for the remaining traders, although longer intervals may be prescribed for least-developed countries.

The TPR process has helped countries assess their trade and economic reforms, and may have contributed to some portion of the liberalisation that has taken place under the Uruguay Round. In the future, the TPR process will help WTO Members evaluate their implementation of the Agreements, as well as provide an early warning of trends of potential concern to all participants in the trading system.

Chapter 31

Migration and Development

Migration and development is a growing area of interest. There has been much debate on the negative impacts of migration on development and vice-versa. On the one hand, it is argued that underdevelopment is a cause of migration, and on the other that migration causes developing countries to lose their highly skilled nationals.

While there is a measure of truth in each of these assertions, properly managed international migration holds enormous potential for the development of countries. Remittances have become a prominent source of external funding for developing countries that surpass official development assistance. In 2005, over US $100 billion were sent home in remittances by migrants, helping to sustain the economies of many developing countries. The total amount of resource remitted may even be two or three times higher, since a large number of transactions are carried out through informal channels. Migration can thus contribute to the reduction of poverty at the local and national level, and to a reduction in the economic vulnerability of developing countries.

Migration may be detrimental to the community of origin if the labour market is depleted by the departure of its most productive and/or qualified members ("brain drain"). However, migrants who have developed and improved their skills abroad can be actors of the "brain gain" by transferring and infusing knowledge, skills and technology into their countries, of origin.

In addition, remittances sent home by migrants can be used to sustain development. The challenge is to develop mechanisms to mitigate as much as possible the negative effects of "brain drain" and to encourage the return of qualified nationals resulting "brain gain".

It should also be noted that in a globalized world, migration is increasingly circular. While many migrants still make a permanent move with their families, an increasing proportion of migratory movements are temporary in nature. Increasingly, countries of origin expect migrants to maintain financial, cultural and sometimes political links with their home country, which may be difficult to reconcile with the expectation for migrants to integrate, on the part of the host country.

In order to benefit from remittances, skills transfer and investment opportunities, it is necessary to create and maintain links between migrants and their potential by encouraging them to contribute human and financial capital to the development of their home communities.

Through advances in communications technology and the decline in travel costs, globalization has made it easier for migrants to stay in contact with their country of origin and to establish lasting links with diasporas and transnational networks.

In the past, states and the international community formulated and implemented separate policies on poverty reduction, globalization, security, refugees and migration, with sometimes different or even conflicting objectives.

Better results can be achieved by considering the close interrelationship between migration and development on national and international levels through coherent and coordinated development and migration polices, and between humanitarian assistance and development assistance. Migration polices dealing with the migration-development nexus include facilitating voluntary return and reintegration, either temporary or permanent, particularly of the highly skilled. Other policies address the transfer of remittances, the reduction of transfer costs and investment in the country of origin by diasporas and returning migrants.

It is also necessary to promote and enhance dialogue and cooperation and the national level between different government agencies as well as at the international level. The aim is to ensure that migration contributes to sustainable development, and that in turn development endeavours to contribute to the management of migration.

In recent years, migration has been making its way steadily to the top of the international agenda, and now calls insistently and urgently for the attention of all governments, regard less of their past involvement or interest in the management of migratory processes.

Migratory flows today are more diverse and complex, with more temporary and circular migration. World demographics, economic, political and social trends mean that governments and societies will need to put more emphasis on migration management in all of its dimensions.

If properly managed, migration can be beneficial for all states and societies. If left unmanaged, it can lead to the exploitation of individual migrations, particularly through human trafficking and migrant smuggling, and be a source of social tension, insecurity and bad relations between nations.

Effective management is required to maximize the positive effects of migration and minimize potentially negative consequences. It is essential to establish orderly and safe migration opportunities while ensuring respect for the integrity of national, sovereign borders. Migration management strategies need to result in the implementation of policies; laws and regulations that take into account the rights and obligations of migrations as well as the social and economic interests of nations and responsibilities of governments.

Over the past decades governments have tended to focus on isolated elements of migration and have thus developed ad-hoc strategies to protect their interests. For some, labour migration needs have predominated, for others asylum has been the main concern. However, to be effective, migration management strategies need to address migration in a comprehensive manner. Governments over the past decades have tended to focus on isolated elements of migration. The challenge today is to shift from an isolate and largely in effective focus to more meaningful, constructive and comprehensive approaches.

At the same time, it is necessary to identify, define and address the fundamental policy issues in the migration debates. This is a tall assignment, since the migratory landscape is complex and rapidly evolving, with challenges emerging at every step of the way.

Most governments are just beginning to develop coherent and comprehensive migration management strategies. There is still a need to better understand migration interests and priorities and to develop a common migration language. Regular dialogue between governments that allows an exchange of experience and the development of new initiatives and approaches to migration management is therefore essential.

Chapter 32

Asian Values Versus Western Democracy
The Pressures of Modernisation

Democracy in Asia is different from Western models. Often, it is only on paper while real power is wielded by autocratic governments. But with the growing integration into the world economy and rising prosperity, the people in Asia are demanding more participation and democratic freedoms.

Democracy has become a talking point also in Asia. Both within and outside the region, more and more people are asking if democracy as the prevailing political system and way of life could not be realised there, too. If it has taken Asia quite a while to get a debate on democracy underway, there are at least two reasons for the delay. First, initial approaches to democracy suffered a setback with the bloody crushing of the Chinese students' movement of Beijing's Tiananmen Square in 1989. That blow also affected the democracy movement beyond China's borders, and it is only gradually recovering from it. Second, the social preconditions for democratic development must, of course, be created. But apparently that is increasingly being done.

Democracy is certainly already a common political system in Asia. India is regarded as the world's biggest democracy. Democracy as a way of choosing the government and participation of the people in political decisions is also at least formally in place in Sri Lanka, Pakistan, the Philippines, Thailand, South Korea, Japan and Mongolia. Even in Singapore, Malaysia and Indonesia, the regimes seek to legitimise their political systems as independent, 'non-western' forms of democracy. So there is no simple answer to the question of democracy in Asia. A number of factors have to be taken into account.

Democracy and Culture

Asia is not only the world's biggest and most populous continent, but also has its greatest cultural, religious and linguistic disversity. The debate on whether Asia is capable of democracy must therefore include the cultural aspect in particular. And that calls for getting to grips with many cliches and prejudices. One of the best-known cliches, trotted out by politicians and intellectuals both within and outside the region, is the assertion that Asia's different quality of life stands in the way of introducing the 'western' concept of democracy there. The prime ministers of Singapore and Malaysia, as well as, of course, the Chinese leadership, have long lauded 'Asian values'. They say these values are fundamentally opposed to the western concept of government and society, which is why the latter could not be realised in an Asian context. The American political scientist Samuel Huntington reinforced this line with his projection of a coming 'clash of cultures'. But no matter how prominent its proponents are they do not give the assertion any more credence. Not least in Asia itself, more and more voices revealed the touting of 'Asian values' to be the attempt to ruling elites to safeguard their power and deny the people political participation.

At any rate, democracy can also in Asia be defined in terms of international and now widely accepted criteria in the sense of a liberal political system. That concrete implementation and building of institutions must respect local conditions is not disputed. A look at Asian culture shows that roots for democracy are most certainly to be found in the region. The South Korean politician Kim Dae

Jung, for example, cites tenets of ancient Chinese philosophy which siad the will of the people must be understood and respected as the will of Heaven. Individual rights to freedom are certainly compatible with Chinese culture. True, it would be going too far to interpret Confucianism as a source of democratic ideals. But there is no doubt that in its cognitive and ehtical systems classical Confucianism was a culture of learning, rationality and justice.

This is the foundation of what is probably the most stable democracy in Asia, that of Japan. There, a kind of philosophical pragmatism linked harmoniously the traditions of Confucianism, Buddhism, Shintoism and Christianity to form the base on which to build a new 'state philosophy'. And even in India, with its great ethnic and cultural diversity, the Westminster model of parliamentary democracy is linked without difficulty with the tradition of Hinduism. Thus, it is possible to connect the caste system, despite all its blatant social injustice, with a political culture which places remarkably great importance on holding elections. In Pakistan and Bangladesh, democratic processes have not only been introduced in Islamic countries, but especially surprisingly—their first democratic governments were led by women. That is also a telling argument against the Asian culture cliche. The case of South Korea shows in turn how in a relatively short period, transparency of government action, growing influence of public opinion, women's access to work, and independence of the judiciary have become established as largely acknowledged standards. In Europe, that took centuries.

In addition, the recent history of Asian countries has not indicated that striving for harmony and shunning disobedience, dissent and conflict are fixed elements of Asian culture. From the turn of the century, there was growing resistance against the colonial powers and local rulers in India, China, former Malaya, Indonesia and elsewhere in the region. And right up to the 1960s there were in many places strong Communist parties or movements which staged protests upto military action both inside and outside their countries. Authoritarian regimes instrumentalise the Asians' alleged need for harmony for ideological purposes. And some western observers readily fall for that subterfuge out of laziness or ignorance.

Economy and Democracy

The transformation processes of the last decade have shown that the reasons for a change of political system and the stabilisation of democracy are many-sided, and can differ from country to country. For example, economic declilne or success can lead equally to democracy or the shattering of it. Contrary to the earlier assumptions of democratic modernisation, we now know that successful economic development is not necessarily a precondition for democracy. In Asia, that is shown quite clearly by the examples of the Philippiness and Monogolia, where turning to democracy appeared to be the way out of a desperate economic situation. On the other hand, the cases of South Korea and Taiwan prove that in the wake of economic improvement more and more people prefer a democratic system, more personal freedom and chances of political participation. The reverse appears to be the case in Singapore, Malaysia and Indonesia, because economic growth there was accompanied by a consolidation of authoritarian structures or establishment of merely formal democracies. The two most stable democracies in Asia are Japan and India.

Supports of Democratic Development

Democracy everywhere needs classes of supporters that stimulate political change and stand in the wings as an alternative government. In Asia, there is now broad agreement that in social market economy countries, economic modernisation leads to a differentiation in their societies that is a precondition for pluralism and democratic development. Above all, the emergence and strengthening of an urban middle class in the Asian democracies is of great significance. But the upper class also plays an important role in enabling democracy. Thus, democratic stability in Thailand depends to a great degree on the government and upper class coming to terms with each other, as well as inclusion of the middle class in the political process. In Thailand, and also in the Philippines, Taiwan and South Korea, democratisation was accompanied by economic liberalisation and cutbacks in government regulation of commerce and industry. It was probably no coincidence that in these countries the economic structural adjustment process of the beginning of the 1980s was followed by a wave of democratisation, which surged from the end of the decade. As in Thailand, Taiwan's focus on exports triggered the rise of small and medium-sised enterprises and a gradually strengthening middle class.

In contrast, commerce and industry in Singapore, Malaysia and Indonesia is subject to considerable government control. If the middle classes which emerged on the back of these countries' economic development fail to call for political participation, that is certainly not only because their governments fulfill their expectations on distribution, convincingly portray the ruling systems as 'authentic democracy' and are skilful in mobilising resentments against alleged destabilisation attempts by the 'West'. Rather, the upper class and the new middle classes also remain politically weak because transformation to the market economy is greatly dependent on government investment. They cannot take on the role of promoters and supporters of democratisation. Where pro-democratic forces are vulnerable to a government's many options of applying sanctions, they remain weak. If the government, as in Singapore, controls 90 per cent of the housing market, rules society with a firm hand, and has a decisive influence on commerce and industry, there are few possibilities of escaping the grip of repression by seeking refuge in a private sector

The situation is similar in Malaysia and Indonesia, where the weakness of the middle class is linked with the fact that most graduates of senior high schools and universities take jobs in the public sector. In Indonesia, the Pancasila ideology of national unity in proving less and less suited to establish social cohesion. The country's entrepreneurs depend to a great degree on government business. In political terms, compared with the Sukarno family's plutocracy they play only the role of 'substitute capitalists'. However, events in South Korea and Taiwan, whose regimes have indeed long been legitimised essentially only by their economic performance, suggest that it is not possible to repress social pluralism and growing demands for participation in the long term.

A strengthening of civil society organisations has been noted in many Asian countries in recent years. It would certainly not be too bold to forecast that these organisations will promote not only economic liberalisation, but also political opening. The nation-wide trade union strike actions in South Korea at the turn of this year were a clear signal in this, direction. They proved that pressures for more participation and better social and working conditions increase along with economic growth. The countries of Southeast Asia must expect something similar, which is why some still shy away from further political liberalisation.

In Singapore, Malaysia and Indoneisa, an additional factor hinders the development of democracy. It is one which in probably no other Asian country, except perhaps for India, carries so much weight. This is the multi-ethnic composition of their societies and its associated potential for conflict. The elites of these countries fear ethnic or religious clashes that could have destabilising impacts. However, it is uncertain how long a certain ethnic group can asset a claim to sole power. That applies, for example, to the bumiputras, the 'Sons of the Earth' in Malaysia. In India, not even the caste system can guarantee the Brahmins their privileged status for ever. In this context, the Philippines government has drawn attention in recent years. It has not only linked economic prosperity with political liberality, but also peacefully settled its conflict with the Moslem minority on Mindanao and integrated them in the pluralistic and democratic state system.

Weak Democratic Institutions

In many Asian countries, democratic institutions are so far only weakly developed. There are in many places only the beginnings of a functioning separation of powers. Parliaments are often almost without significance in the face of strong presidents or bureaucracies. The judiciary is often subject to direct government influence, and corruption is a widespread evil. Even in the established democracies of India and Thailand, massive buying of votes is routine. True, there are now multi-party system in most countries of the region. But, except mainly for India and Japan, the parties are weak on organisation and often aligned more on a charismatic leader than on a programme.

China and Indochina

Although the Chinese and Vietnamese Communist Party congresses in the autumn of this year, particularly Beijing's took more strides towards economic opening, they confirmed forecasts that political doors would remain closed. Only the beginnings of a civil society or expectations of political participation can be noted there. In Vietnam, for example, there have been indications of the emergence of forms of civil society organisations since the regime realised that the state alone cannot provide the necessary development inputs. In addition, with their opening to foreign investment, new legal structures have begun to develop in both countries which hold out the long-term prospect of winning room for manoeuvre from the state arbitrary rule.

On the other hand, the case of Cambodia shows how difficult it is to introduce democracy after 20 years of civil-war if the social prerequisites for it have not yet been created. The brutalising of political culture, a poor level of education, immense social and economic problems, antagonistic political structures, and anyway, the absence of a supporting class, greatly impedes democratic development. That certainly also applies to Burma.

Eternal Demands for Democracy?

Unlike other regions, the robust self-confidence of the Asian tiger economies and their lesser dependence on western development assistance leads them to reject external demands for democratic processes and organisations to be established in non-democratic countries as undesired interference in their internal affairs. Japan, the region's largest donor and investor, has in any case no such ambitions. Nevertheless, in most Asian countries there are signs of a growing interest in a socio-political dialogue and exchange of experience. The mechanisms of the past are increasingly being differentiated for organisational purposes, and complex societies are apparently more and more being perceived as insufficient. New social issues in the context of economic modernisation, new security policy tasks in the shadow of China's growing military strength, and new environmental burdens are sparking increasing interest in an international exchange of experience. The continuing economic prosperity that Asian countries are expected to enjoy, at least in the medium term, and their further integration in the world market will probably fuel even more their people's expectations of political participation, thus also promoting the development of democracy.

Chapter 33

Promotion of Industry and Foreign Investment in Africa

For more than a decade now industrialisation focusing on the promotion of private sector initiative and the encouragement of foreign investment has been given high rank in economic development policy by the authorities in most African countries. Yet, none of these have materialised with any significant impact in most of Sub-Saharan Africa. Consequently, an atmosphere of general disappointment and even discouragement with African industrialisation is spreading, increasing some doubts whether adopted policies and programmes are worth being pursued. This is certainly not a constructive environment and calls for a revision of assumptions, expectations and the means employed, in order to set more realistic and attainable prospects.

After independence, governments usually took a strong stand in regulating the economy and involved themselves in setting up and controlling a great number of state-owned enterprises. Preference was given to large and often capital-intensive enterprises either in production of basic consumer goods for the domestic markets or primary production and processing of export commodities. The role of private industry was relatively neglected or left without clear incentives to operate in the import substitution small and medium sized enterprises (SME) sector. A sceptical, sometimes hostile, attitude prevailed towards foreign investment which was usually controlled and regulated by restrictive concessions and investment laws.

In the early 1980s it had to be recognised that these policies were rather unsuccessful and could hardly be sustained. Growing budget deficits, high foreign debt and reduced flows of foreign credit imposed a revision of previous orientations. Structural adjustment policies were designed and gradually pursued. They basically implied:

- a general reduction of state control of economies;
- liberalisation of internal markets and opening to international competition;
- market adjustment of currency exchange mechanisms;
- deliberate opening to foreign investment;
- privatisation of state-owned enterprises and promotion of private enterprise in general.

Disappointing Results

However, what are the factual results to-date? Basically, all the global performance data show a rather bleak picture for Sub-Saharan Africa in recent years, especially in comparison to other developing regions. Real annual GDP growth barely reached 1.5 per cent and growth of manufacturing industry has not significantly improved. Hence the GDP contribution of manufacturing industry remains below 15 per cent in most countries. Sub-Saharan Africa's share of total export volume stagnates and is the lowest of all developing regions. Exports continue to contain mostly primary commodities and only some 10 per cent of manufactured products. Compared with other regions. Africa continues with the lowest rate of private investment (some 8 per cent of GDP in 1995). Whereas Latin America and East Asia attract together about 80 per cent of net foreign direct investment to developing regions, the African share fluctuates between 1 and 2 per cent.

Constraints and Opportunities

The major constraints for advanced industrialisation in Africa can be briefly recalled:

Restricted Size of Domestic Markets

This is of prime importance for foreign investment which predominantly seeks access and expansion into new markets. But also for local investors, it is a serious obstacle as certain technologies and industrial units need a substantial market size to achieve economies of scale. Regional market integration, often advocated as a desirable solution, has not made significant progress for various, apparently quite persistent reasons (of which economic nationalism is one, and not only in Africa).

Comparatively High Factor Cost

Besides labour cost and productivity, which are not a decisive advantage in Africa in comparison to other developing regions, the shortage of skilled manpower with industrial experience, as well as infrastructural environment and logistics and generally a lack of integration (inter-sectoral linkage) are restricting factors.

Scarcity of Foreign Exchange

The general shortage of foreign exchange and the exchange rate fluctuations create major obstacles and uncertainties, especially for local market oriented industries which typically depend strongly on imported inputs. This also seriously restricts investment finance which often has to be contracted, and repaid, in foreign currency.

Lack of Financial Resources

Equity capital resources of African entrepreneurs are generally quite limited, and medium to long-term bank loans are constrained by low savings ratios and restrictive conditions of the banking sector.

Limiting Number of Industrial Entrepreneurs

Most entrepreneurs in African countries are found in the artisanal and small industry sector, whereas the small number of potential investors with the financial strength for medium to large enterprise comes from a trading and service background. The latter are usually led by a short-term profit motive and lack to some extent the relevant management experience for industrial enterprise.

Large-Scale Enterprises with Investments above Some ECU 5 Million

If we call this category large, this of course is in relation to the context in most African countries: what is "large" there, might well be considered medium or small-sized from an industrialised country stand point and that is part of the dilemma. Typically, in this category, one finds mining and mineral exploitation companies, agricultural commodity production and primary processing enterprises, mostly geared towards export markets furthermore, some industries predominantly in food, beverages, textile and construction materials branches producing for local or sometimes regional markets.

The number of enterprises in this range is not more than a few dozens in most countries and only a few new investment opportunities are appearing or could be envisaged. This is rather a domain where many existing companies are state-owned and are seeking privatisation, or where some of the private-owned companies require rehabilitation and restructuring in order to face competitive market conditions.

With some exceptions there is a general tendency of multinational investors to get less involved in standard commodity production; and further processing of primary mineral and agricultural products is maintained closer to the markets in industrialised countries rather than being shifted to primary producing countries. Hence, for the traditional resource-based industries with export orientation, there will be some scope for quantitative expansion, but rather little real prospect for local further processing and linkage with domestic economies.

Large, local market-oriented enterprises will continue to be constrained by limited domestic purchasing power, lack of international competitiveness and a serious shortage of foreign exchange, the latter so much more when they require high import contents. There is usually little scope for a multiplication and diversification in this domain, as often one single enterprise unit covers the entire domestic demand (like petroleum refineries, cement factories, cereal mills, breweries, textile mills). If they present some attraction to private, also foreign investment, this still is often conditioned by protection allowing quasimonopolistic market positions.

Small and Medium-sized Enterprises (SMEs)

The great majority of manufacturing enterprises is in this category. It is basically composed of import substitution activities mostly for local consumer goods, some production and processing of local inputs for export (e.g. non-traditional agro-products like vegetables and flowers, woodbased products, processed fish) and some labour-intensive manufacturing, typically under free-zone status. There are only a few enterprises producing intermediate or investment goods for the local market (like metal and construction material industries).

As recently evidenced in several African countries (e.g. in Ghana, Zimbabwe and Uganda), considerable growth potential exists and some investment can be mobilised for SMEs. Non-traditional exports provide good opportunities, especially as they earn foreign exchange. Free-zone industries have some potential in selected countries, as already known from Mauritius and indicated by more recent trends, e.g., in Madagascar and Cape Verde. But the core potential for SMEs remains probably in domestic markets, which involves the challenge for selective import substitution, where it can be efficient, and for the processing of local materials, with appropriate technologies and unit sizes for the basic local demand.

Perspectives for International Cooperation

Many of the leading multilateral and bilateral development institutions have adopted policies and are providing programmes, mechanisms and resources to assist the development of industry in Africa, to facilitate private foreign investment as well as various forms of enterprise partnership. The World Bank Group has been particularly active in this domain by creating over the last ten years specialised facilities like the Foreign Investment Advisory Service (FIAS), the African Project Development Facility (APDF), the African Management Services Company and the Africa Enterprise Fund (AEF) through which the International Finance Corporation provides direct investment funding to medium-sized companies. The European Union put strong emphasis on private enterprise and investment in the fourth Lome Convention and besides institutional assistance towards a better legislative and administrative environment, offers a comprehensive range of financial and technical support to enterprises. The number of projects implemented by the European Commission, especially geared to small-scale industry by way of technical assistance, credit lines and guarantee funds has grown significantly.

Financial resources managed by the EIB, especially risk capital provided from the European Development Fund, were strongly increased and a significant portion has been devoted to investment in the private sector. Some new mechanisms were introduced to make the use of risk capital more flexible and suitable for direct financing of larger projects and indirect financing of SMEs via local credit institutions. The Centre for the Development of Industry (CDI) has been strengthened for its tasks to promote EU-ACP enterprise partnerships and to support the creation or improvement of SMEs. It is noteworthy that CDI can offer its range of practical services directly to individual investors and existing enterprises.

Hence it appears that, although private foreign investors for Africa are scarce, there is no scarcity of external means and mechanisms to assist African enterprise. Yet there is probably a need to better adapt the means to prevailing conditions, to orientate them with clearer priorities towards effective growth potentials and to coordinate them for higher efficiency.

Bibliography

A.K. Sen, "Pattern of British Enterprise in India: 1854-1914" in *Social and Economic Development,* B. Singh and V.B. Singh, (eds), New Delhi, 1965, p. 420

Ashton B., Hill, K., Piazza A. and R. Zeita, "Famine in China, 1958-61", *Population and Development Review* 10, 1985, pp. 613-45.

Blyn George, *Agricultural Trends in India—1891-1947* University of Pennsylvania Press, 1966.

Brodkin E.I., "Proprietary Mutations and the Mutiny in Rohilkhand", *Journal of Asian Studies,* XXVIII, No. 4, August 1969, p. 667.

Cohn Bernard, "The Initial British Impact on India," *Journal of Asian Studies,* XIV, No. 4, August 1960, p. 418.

Cottrel P.L., British *Overseas Investment in the Nineteenth Century,* Macmillan, 1975.

Das Parekh and Parekh, *India Development Report* (1999), Oxford University Press. .

Domar, Evsey, *The Theory of Economic Growth*, MIT Press, 1966.

Fairbank John, *China,* Harvard University Press, 1963.

For Details See Swamy Subramanian, "Structural Changes and the Distribution of Income by Size: The Case of India", *Review of Income and Wealth*, June 1967.

For Estimates, see Rostow, W.W., *Prospects for Communist China,* Wiley, New York, 1954.

Frank Andre Gunder, "India in the World Economy, 1400-1750", *Economic and Political Weekly,* July 27, 1999.

Goldsmith Raymond, *The Financial Development of India: 1860-1977,* Oxford University Press, 1983, p. 47.

In 1835, Lord Macaulay prepared a *Minute on Education* Which Became the Basis for English Language Education in India of *Journal of Asian Studies,* XVII, No. 4, August 1958, p. 570.

Jayal Niraja Gopal, "The Governance Agenda", *Economic and Political Weekly,* Feb. 22, 1997.

Kuhn Phillip, "Local Taxation and Finance in Republican China" in Jones, Susan (ed): *Select Papers from the Centre for Far Eastern Studies,* The University of Chicago, 1972.

Murphy Rhoads; *The Outsiders: Western Experience in India and China,* Univ. of Michigan Press, 1977.

Perkins Dwight H. (ed.), *China's Modern Development in Historical Perspective,* Stanford, 1975.

Raychaudhari T., "The Mid-Eighteenth Century Background" in *The Cambridge Economic History of India,* Vol. II, Cambridge University Press, 1982 (Henceforth: CEHI)

Reich Robert (ed.), *The Power of Public Ideas, Ballinger,* Cambridge, Mass USA, 1988.

See Report of the Destruction of Industries in North China, Chinese Delegation to the United Nations, 1948, New York.

Stokes Eric, *English Utilitarians and India* Clarendon Press, 1959, p. 134.

Subramanian S., *A Statistical Summary of the Social and Economic Trends in India* (In the Inter-War Period), Office of the Economic Adviser, Government of India, New Delhi, 1945, Table VI.

Swamy Subramanian, *Government-Academia Interface,* Paper Presented at the Prime Minister's Consultative Conference at Namibia, February 26, 1997.

Swamy Subramanian, *Spectral Analysis of Indian Prices: 1860-1967* in Bhatt, Mahesh and Mukund Trivedi (eds),

Liberalism and Less Developed Countries, Gujarat University.

Swamy Subramanian, *Investement Policy in the Indian Economy,* Paper Presented at the University of Bolognia, Italy, September 1992.

Swamy Subramanian, Response to Economic Challenges: The Economic History of China and India (1870-1950)", *Quarterly Journal of Economics* (1979).

Swamy Subramanian, *Economic Growth in China and India [1870-1986]: A Comparison in Perspective,* UBS, New Delhi, 1989.

Swamy Subramanian, *Eonomic Growth in China and India: A Comparative Appraisal-1952-70,* University of Chicago Press, 1973.

Index